Collins

Enhanced Engaging English 8

Workbook

Name: ______________________________

Grade: ________ Section: __________

Preeti Roychoudhury
Sadeqa Rahman Siddiqui

HarperCollins*Publishers*

Publishing operations in 17 countries and 120+ imprints globally

William Collins' dream of knowledge for all began with the publication of his first book in 1819. A self-educated mill worker, he not on enriched millions of lives, but also founded a flourishing publishing house. Today, staying true to this spirit, Collins books are packe with inspiration, innovation and practical expertise. They place you at the centre of a world of possibility and give you exactly what yc need to explore it.

Published by Collins Learning
An imprint of HarperCollins*Publishers* India
Building No. 10, Tower A, 4th Floor, DLF Cyber City, Gurugram, Haryana 122002, India

First edition: 2025
Reprint: 10 9 8 7 6 5 4 3 2 1
ISBN: 978-93-6569-669-1
Printed and bound in India by MicroPrints India, New Delhi

Browse the complete Collins catalogue at www.collins.in.
For any queries/feedback, please write to us at SCHOOLSUPPORT@harpercollins.co.in.

Preface

Enhanced Engaging English aims to instill an appreciation for literature in today's learners, while equipping them with the tools to develop native fluency and communicative competence in using the English language. The eight-level series comprises Coursebooks, Workbooks, and digital resources for teachers for all levels.

The revised edition has been aligned closely with the guidelines of the National Curriculum Framework, 2023 through its focus on twenty-first century skills, Sustainable Development Goals (SDGs), cross-curricular learning, 'Happiness' content and art-integrated learning. Coursebooks and Workbooks 1 and 2 integrate the essence of NIPUN (National Initiative for Proficiency in Reading with Understanding and Numeracy). They aim to motivate students to read independently, improve their vocabulary, develop their critical thinking and creative skills and enhance their ability to express themselves verbally and in writing.

The lessons are built around carefully selected literary pieces with distinct cross-curricular themes, and presented with glossary, explanation of literary terms and interesting trivia. The end-of-chapter exercises address the needs of formal language learning.

The **Workbooks** are designed to complement the Coursebooks, by providing additional skills practice, review and assessments. They comprise the following sections:

Comprehension includes factual, inferential and evaluative questions based on short reading passages.

Way with Words includes exercises on the vocabulary topics encountered in the Coursebook as well as extension activities derived from it. It also incorporates activities on literary devices and figures of speech, spelling drills and exercises on dictionary usage.

Grammar in Use starts with a short explanation of important grammar concepts covered in the Coursebook, followed by plenty of practice for reinforcement.

Listening and Speaking builds students' oral and aural communication skills. It includes tasks such as phonics drills, conversation practice, role plays and debates to develop spoken English skills. Listening comprehension exercises teach students to listen for both general and specific details. In poetry chapters, there are activities on stress, rhyme and metre.

Pen it Down: The activities in this section include guided and free writing tasks derived from the reading text, which build on the functional and creative writing skills of the learner.

Each Workbook also contains two **Tests**. One of these is based on the principle of SAFAL (Structured Assessment For Analyzing Learning), a competency-based assessment introduced by CBSE. They assess the competencies of critical thinking as well as inquiry-based and analysis-based learning. The other test is modelled on class assessments.

The series encourages competency-based education which allows concept acquisition at the learner's own pace, based on individual ability. We hope that it will foster a love for literature and reading in young learners.

Detailed Contents

Unit	Themes	Way with Words	Grammar in Use	Listening and Speaking	Pen it Down
1. Where the Mind is Without Fear	Our Country	• Homophones and homographs • Metaphors	• Order of adjectives • Relative pronouns	• Group discussion on a given topic	• Essay writing
2. The River Came Home	Town and Country	• Word families • Words describing character and personality	• Types of sentences and their transformation • Conditional sentences • Forming abstract nouns from verbs and adjectives	• Enacting an interview	• Formal letter
3. Felling of the Banyan Tree	Conservation	• Contextual usage • Idioms related to plants	• Reflexive pronouns • Subject-verb agreement	• Group discussion on a given topic	• Formal letter
4. The Monkey's Paw	Horror Fiction	• Words related to horror • Idioms related to fear	• Modals	• Pair discussion on a given topic	• Diary entry
5. The Road Not Taken	Making Choices	• Words with multiple meanings • Idioms and phrases about choice	• Types of adverbs • Phrases and clauses	• Listening comprehension: answering questions • Reading a poem with correct stress and intonation	• Email writing
6. A Tale of Two Cities	Hard Times	• Transformation of parts of speech • Word meanings	• Transformation of sentences • Adjectives: changing degrees of comparison	• Describing a scene	• Essay writing
7. Ozymandias	Past and Present	• Metonymy and synecdoche • Words indicating size • Idioms with *hand* and *heart*	• Prepositions • Prepositional phrases	• Debate on a given topic	• Writing an autobiography
8. The Monk Protectors of Arunachal's Wetlands	Environment	• Collocations	• Active and passive voice	• Listening comprehension: fill in the blanks	• Précis writing
9. Elder Brother	Self and Family	• Synonyms and antonyms	• Main and subordinate clauses	• Pair work: enacting a conversation	• Argumentative essay
Test Paper					

Unit	Themes	Way with Words	Grammar in Use	Listening and Speaking	Pen it Down
10. The Rime of the Ancient Mariner	Sea Travel	• Using *give* and *take* • Archaisms	• Types of subordinate clauses: adjective, adverb, and noun • Complex sentences	• Metre and feet: scanning • Spin-a-Yarn: saying stories using prompts	• Writing the ending of a story
11. The Six Napoleons	Mystery and Detection	• Words from detective fiction • Types of books	• Direct and indirect speech	• Listening comprehension: multiple choice questions	• Story writing
12. The Commentator	Sport	• Idioms with *talk* • Words related to football	• Tenses	• Conversation: making an apology	• Paragraph writing • Making a poster
13. The Gift of the Magi	Love and Sacrifice	• Idioms related to money • Suffixes	• Using *for*, *during* and *while* • Question tags • Subordinating conjunctions	• Listening comprehension: answering questions	• Reviewing a book • Writing an alternate ending to a story
14. The Last Wolf	Man and Nature	• Contextual usage • Idioms related to animals	• Joining sentences: participles	• Class discussion on a given topic	• Report writing
15. A Short Walk in the Hindu Kush	In Faraway Lands	• Contextual usage • Compound adjectives	• Infinitives and gerunds	• Pair work: enacting a conversation	• Picture composition • Making a travel brochure
16. Refugee Blues	War and Peace	• Using suffixes to form nationalities • Words of foreign origin	• Determiners: quantifiers and distributives • Punctuation	• Listening comprehension: true/false	• Writing a newspaper report • Writing a poem
17. My Financial Career	Humour	• Idioms related to anxiety • Similar sounding words	• Transformation of sentences	• Listening comprehension: multiple choice questions	• Process writing
18. The Tragedy of Julius Caesar	Ancient History	• Irony • Archaic sentences • Understatement	• Simple, compound, and complex sentences • Joining sentences with correlative conjunctions	• Reciting a speech from the play and explaining it	• Writing a speech • Writing a notice
Assessment (SAFAL)					

Contents

1

Where the Mind is Without Fear

Way with Words

Homophones and Homographs

Words with the same pronunciation which may have different spellings and meanings are called **homophones**.

Examples: bye – buy, new – knew

A. Tick (✓) the correct options to complete the sentences.

1. A (cache/cash) of weapons was discovered when the army raided the safe house.
2. All letters sent home by the soldiers went through a strict (censor/sensor).
3. You must retain the (receipt/reseat) for the items you have bought if you wish to exchange them later.
4. There was a (taut/taught) expression on her face when she was being questioned about the missing jewellery case.
5. There was no (colonel/kernel) of truth in his arguments.
6. The (barren/baron) land produced nothing last year.
7. Will you help me (draught/draft) my job application?

Words that have the same spelling, but different meanings and pronunciation are called **homographs**.

Example: minute (1. each of the 60 parts of an hour, that are equal to 60 seconds
2. extremely small)

B. A homograph has been underlined in each of the following sentences. Make another sentence with the homograph to show a different meaning.

1. This market is famous for fresh <u>produce</u> and is very popular with the locals.

____

____

2. The <u>compound</u> was filled with children waving flags and singing the National Anthem.

____

____

3. He did not <u>bat</u> an eyelid when he lied to his mother about the punishment he had got.

____

____

4. The <u>monitor</u> of the class can refuse to take responsibility for what happens in his absence.

____

____

5. Sometimes, an unkind word can <u>wound</u> more than an actual blow.

____

____

METAPHORS

A **metaphor** is a figure of speech in which a person or thing is compared to another, otherwise unrelated person or thing by stating that they are the same in a particular way.

Example: Varun is a night owl.

C. Underline the metaphor in each sentence and explain its usage.

1. People flooded into the stadium as soon as the gates opened.

____

____

2. War time requires people to tighten their belts as resources are suddenly scarce.

____

____

3. His half-baked idea of opening a jewellery business at the edge of the town was bound to end in failure.

____

____

4. The news of his father's illness was the last straw on the camel's back for Peter.

____

____

5. The road ahead was a ribbon stretching across the desert.

____

____

6. A ripple of laughter went through the auditorium as the comedian messed up his lines again.

____

____

7. He was met with a wall of silence when he began asking questions about the existence of his grandfather's will.

____

____

Grammar in Use

Order of Adjectives

When multiple adjectives are placed before a noun, they usually follow a particular order. Adjectives which describe opinions or attitudes are usually placed first, before fact-based adjectives.

Examples: He was modelling a **comfortable fur** shrug.
It was an **incredibly large broad-backed young blue Indian** whale.

Look at this table which shows the general order of adjectives.

Order	Relating to	Examples
1.	opinion	*incredible, astonishing*
2.	size	*big, small*
3.	physical quality	*narrow, broad*
4.	shape	*square, spherical*
5.	age	*young, elderly*
6.	colour	*pink, yellow, blue*
7.	origin	*Indian, Korean, European*
8.	material	*steel, wooden*
9.	purpose	*moulding, cleaning, rubbing*

A. Arrange the adjectives in the following sentences in the correct order.

1. We were rudely woken up by our (red/small/alarm) clock.

____

2. Maya bought a (yellow/nice/cotton) dress for the birthday party.

____

3. We saw an (old/African/interesting/wooden) bowl at the museum.

____

4. We spotted a (beautiful/new/huge) sailing boat far in the sea.

____

5. Shall we buy this (black/smart/leather) jacket for our cousin?

____

6. We are taught English by a (wise/American/old) gentleman.

____

Relative Pronouns

Relative pronouns refer to nouns mentioned before them in a sentence. They are **who, whom, whose, which,** and **that**.

Examples: This is the friend **whose** cycle I am borrowing.
This is the house **which** my grandfather had built.

B. Complete the sentences with suitable relative pronouns.

1. Shamita has gone to Gujarat, ____________ is her birthplace.
2. That's Rohit, the boy ____________ has just arrived at the airport.
3. Is this the street ____________ leads to her house?
4. Did you receive the book ____________ I sent yesterday?
5. Geetika, ____________ is my sister, is the tallest girl in her class.
6. The man standing in the corner, ____________ face was hidden behind a mask, took my bag.
7. I liked the present ____________ you sent me.

Listening and Speaking

Jack has recently joined a new school. Read this conversation between Jack and his teacher. Then, discuss his problem in groups and suggest ways to help him out.

Teacher: Jack, may I talk to you about something that is worrying me?

Jack: Yes, Sir.

Teacher: I have noticed that you have stopped going out to play during recess. Is there a problem?

Jack: No Sir, I just prefer to stay alone in the classroom.

Teacher: Jack, tell me if someone is bothering you.

Jack: Actually, there is a boy. He is quite big. Every time he sees me outside the class, he teases me mercilessly and the other students just laugh.

Pen it Down

Tagore dreamt of a free India where people would be liberated not only from foreign rule but social and religious shackles as well. Do you think we have managed to achieve that? Write an essay voicing your opinion on the topic.

2 The River Came Home

Comprehension

Read this famous poem by Alfred, Lord Tennyson.

The Charge of the Light Brigade

Half a league, half a league,
Half a league onward,
All in the valley of Death
Rode the six hundred.

'Forward, the Light Brigade!'
'Charge for the guns!' he said:
Into the valley of Death
Rode the six hundred.
'Forward, the Light Brigade!'
Was there a man dismay'd?
Not tho' the soldier knew
Someone had blunder'd:
Theirs not to make reply,
Theirs not to reason why,
Theirs but to do and die:
Into the valley of Death
Rode the six hundred.

Cannon to right of them,
Cannon to left of them,
Cannon in front of them
Volley'd and thunder'd;
Storm'd at with shot and shell,
Boldly they rode and well,
Into the jaws of Death,
Into the mouth of Hell
Rode the six hundred.

Flash'd all their sabres bare,
Flash'd as they turn'd in air,
Sabring the gunners there,
Charging an army, while
All the world wonder'd:

Plunged in the battery-smoke
Right thro' the line they broke;
Cossack and Russian
Reel'd from the sabre stroke
Shatter'd and sunder'd.
Then they rode back, but not
Not the six hundred.

When can their glory fade?
O the wild charge they made!
  All the world wondered.
Honour the charge they made,
Honour the Light Brigade,
  Noble six hundred.

Answer the questions in a few lines.

1. How many soldiers were there in the Light Brigade?

2. Who were these soldiers fighting?

3. What was the 'blunder'?

4. How did the soldiers react to the 'blunder'? Why?

5. What do the phrases 'Into the jaws of Death,/Into the mouth of Hell' mean?

6. Identify two examples of alliteration from the poem.

7. Explain the meaning of the lines:
   'Forward, the Light Brigade!'
   Was there a man dismay'd?

Way with Words

WORD FAMILIES

Different words are said to belong to the same **word family** when they have the same root word with different prefixes or suffixes attached to it.

Examples: happy happily unhappy unhappiness happiness

A. Make as many words as possible from the following root words. One is done for you.

1. *courage: encourage, discourage, courageous, courageously, encouraging*
2. rest: ____________________
3. help: ____________________
4. care: ____________________
5. peril: ____________________
6. force: ____________________
7. respect: ____________________
8. look: ____________________
9. book: ____________________

WORDS DESCRIBING CHARACTER AND PERSONALITY

B. Read the following passage and underline the adjectives used to describe character.

Yesterday, I moved into my new hostel. Let me tell you about my roommates: Rohit studies history and seems very intelligent and witty. His younger brother, Rohan, however, is simple and good. The fourth person in our group, Derek, is quite a character. He is very reserved and has the most eccentric eating habits. There is also the meddlesome Soham who is our next-door neighbour, but keeps minding everyone else's business. Soham's roommate, the unassuming Balvinder, is also an aspiring musician who has surprised everyone by winning a talent contest.

C. Now, complete the table by matching a few of the character traits from the previous exercise to the idioms given in the box.

a dark horse busybody oddball sharp as a tack salt of the earth

Adjectives	Idioms
1.	
2.	
3.	
4.	
5.	

Grammar in Use

TYPES OF SENTENCES AND THEIR TRANSFORMATION

You know that sentences are of four types:

1. **Assertive sentences** convey a fact or opinion.

Example: Gopala was a quiet fellow.

2. **Interrogative sentences** ask a question.

Example: So you were thinking to buy all those toys in that pile?

3. **Exclamatory sentences** convey an emotion and is accompanied by the exclamation mark at the end of the sentence.

Example: Hurrah! Neeraj Chopra won a gold medal at the Olympics.

4. **Imperative sentences** convey an apology, an order or a request.

Example: Please tell me where he is.

These sentences can be transformed from one form to another.

Examples: Can you wear that dress to the party? (interrogative)
I wonder if you can wear that dress to the party. (assertive)
What a wonderful sight! (exclamatory)
It was a wonderful sight. (assertive)

A. Rewrite the following sentences as instructed.

1. Alas! The dodo is an extinct bird. (assertive sentence)

____

2. What is your name? (assertive sentence)

____

3. I have not seen her at work today. (interrogative sentence)

____

4. The film was very successful. (exclamatory sentence)

____

5. Please shut the door. (assertive sentence)

____

6. Aren't you sorry for your behaviour? (assertive sentence)

____

B. Rewrite the following sentences according to the instructions given in the brackets.

1. Clean the dormitory now. (Begin: The ...)

 ____

 ____

2. How unfortunate that she should treat her elders so rudely! (Rewrite without the exclamation mark.)

 ____

 ____

3. Isn't that the Eiffel Tower in the distance? (Begin: That ...)

 ____

 ____

4. It is a lovely song that she is singing. (Rewrite using the exclamation mark.)

 ____

5. Let the food be served to the guests. (Rewrite as an order.)

 ____

6. Please remember to bring your documents with you. (Use 'forget'.)

 ____

7. This is not the bag I wanted to buy. (Rewrite as a question.)

 ____

Conditional Sentences

Conditional sentences are used to express a situation in which the action in the main clause can take place only if a certain condition is fulfilled. The subordinate clauses depicting the conditions are known as **conditional clauses** or **if clauses**.

Example: If I had known the address, I would have sent her flowers.
Here, the action of sending flowers, in the main clause, would have taken place only if the condition of knowing the address had been fulfilled.

C. Complete the following sentences.

1. If the weather improves ______________________________.
2. We can invite him if ______________________________.
3. Is there any problem if ______________________________?
4. I am not sure if ______________________________.
5. Unless we ensure their safety, ______________________________.
6. They will not reply unless ______________________________.

FORMING ABSTRACT NOUNS FROM VERBS AND ADJECTIVES

D. Abstract nouns can be formed from adjectives and verbs. Complete the table.

Verb	Adjective	Abstract Noun
1. grow		
2.		bravery
3. succeed		success
4.	lively	
5. laugh		

E. Complete the following sentences using the correct forms of the words in brackets.

1. The ________________ farmer spoke well. (honesty)
2. The ________________ was too terrifying for the little girl. (dark)
3. There is little advantage in having so much ________________. (proud)
4. That boy deserves no ________________. (punish)
5. Did the police offer him ________________? (protect)
6. He has several ________________ on the matter. (think)

Listening and Speaking

Work in pairs. Imagine that you are an avid traveller and your partner is a journalist. Carry out an interview where you are being asked about the most wonderful sights you have seen. Change roles after ten questions.

Pen it Down

Imagine that you have discovered a rare species of bird in your neighbourhood. Write a letter to the director of the zoo in your city informing him about it.

Conservation

3
Felling of the Banyan Tree

Way with Words

Contextual Usage

You have learnt that the meanings of some words are sometimes dependent on their contextual usage.
Read this line.
My father told the tenants to leave.
Here, 'leave' means 'to go away'. However, the word 'leaves' also refers to 'the flat green parts of a plant'.

A. These words are from the poem 'Felling of the Banyan Tree'. Frame sentences with them such that they are used in a different sense than their usage in the poem.

1. problem ____________________
2. feet ____________________
3. ground ____________________
4. trunk ____________________
5. axes (plural of 'axis') ____________________

Idioms Related to Plants

B. Match these idioms with their meanings.

Idioms	Meanings
1. flowery speech	a. money used to start a small business
2. olive branch	b. deal with a problem when it is small
3. broken reed	c. not see the whole situation because one is busy with the small details
4. nip something in the bud	d. insubstantial communication
5. seed money	e. the best of a class of things or people
6. can't see the wood for the trees	f. a peace offering
7. the cream of the crop	g. an unreliable support

C. **Use the idioms from the previous exercise in sentences of your own.**

1. ____________________
2. ____________________
3. ____________________
4. ____________________
5. ____________________
6. ____________________
7. ____________________

Grammar in Use

REFLEXIVE PRONOUNS

Reflexive pronouns are used when the action of the subject turns back on the subject itself. These are **myself**, **yourself**, **yourselves**, **himself**, **herself**, **oneself**, **itself**, **ourselves**, and **themselves**.

Example: The boy fixed the fan **himself**.

A. **Complete the sentences with appropriate reflexive pronouns.**

1. Ria is often found talking to ____________
2. Alice collected these shells ____________ from the beaches of Pondicherry.
3. My father can repair his car ____________
4. I wouldn't believe that the film was fantastic till I saw it ____________
5. Parul cut ____________ with a knife while chopping vegetables.
6. The students behaved ____________ when the teacher stepped out of the room.
7. Believe it or not, I wrote this poem ____________!
8. Grandma knitted ____________ a shawl.

SUBJECT-VERB AGREEMENT

The **agreement of subject and verb** means that the verb must agree with the subject in number and person for a sentence to be grammatically correct.

Examples: Each correct answer **is** worth two marks. (singular subject: answer; singular verb: is)
Both women **were** French. (plural subject: women; plural verb: were)

If there are more than one nouns in a sentence, we sometimes mistakenly make the verb agree with the noun nearest it. We should make sure that the verb agrees with the correct subject.

Examples: One of the pies **has spoiled**. [✓]
One of the pies **have spoiled**. [×]

B. Underline the correct options to complete the sentences.

1. Neither you nor I (is/am) available for the party.
2. Harry, together with his friends from Hogwarts, (was/were) present.
3. Curry and noodles (are/is) not a conventional combination.
4. The jury (were/was) divided in their verdict about the innocence of the accused.
5. *Twenty Thousand Leagues Under the Sea* (is/are) one of the most famous books by Jules Verne.
6. Three-fourths of the property (is/are) in his name.
7. A number of rebels (has/have) been jailed.
8. Either my mother or my father (is/are) coming to pick me up.
9. George and Lisa (doesn't/don't) want to go to the opera.
10. Either option (are/is) suitable.
11. My favourite pair of trousers (has/have) shrunk.
12. Every one of my toys (are/is) kept properly.
13. One of my friends (are/is) going to London this year.
14. Computers (is/are) my favourite subject.
15. My grandfather, along with all his pets, (is/are) moving closer to our home.

Listening and Speaking

Think of some of the major environmental changes taking place in your country recently. Have a group discussion on what the causes might be and how they affect the lives of the citizens.

You may talk about the following points:

- rapid urbanization reducing green cover
- frequent oil spills endangering marine life
- mining and excavation leading to loss of habitat for animals

Pen it Down

Imagine that many trees in your neighbourhood park have been felled to make space for a basketball court. Although basketball is your favourite sport, the decision has not made you happy. Write a letter to the editor of your local newspaper expressing your views on the different ways the park can be made fun and engaging for children without felling trees.

Remember to include the following points in your letter:

- the locality of your park
- the existing facilities in the park
- the reasons the trees should remain
- suggestions for making the park a fun place for everyone

Horror Fiction

4
The Monkey's Paw

Way with Words

Words Related to Horror

A. Match the words related to horror in column A to their meanings in column B. Then frame sentences using any four words.

Words	Meanings
1. dread	a. intend to do harm
2. frighten	b. very unpleasant
3. haunted	c. be in fearful anticipation
4. menace	d. cause fear
5. ghastly	e. of or relating to things that cannot be explained according to natural laws
6. supernatural	f. said to be of a place where a ghost regularly appears

____

____

____

____

Idioms Related to Fear

B. Complete the idioms related to fear using the words in the box.

spine	mouth	nerve	daylights	feet	wits

1. Don't play that strange music! It sends shivers down my ____________.
2. She gets cold ____________ every time she is asked to play the piano in front of an audience.
3. My heart was in my ____________ as I opened the envelope.
4. He lost his ____________ when he realised that his plan had backfired.

5. The sight of a tiger's pawprint outside our campsite shook the living __________ out of all of us.
6. The latest stock market news has scared the __________ out of investors.

Grammar in Use

Modals

Modals are auxiliary verbs used to convey specific meanings in particular situations. These are **can, could, will, would, shall, should, may, might, must, dare, need** and **ought to**.

Examples: You **might** get the train if you leave now.
Could I take a break for ten minutes, please?

Remember that modals do not change their form according to the number and person of the subject. They are always followed by a bare infinitive.

A. Choose the correct modal verb from the brackets to complete the sentences.

1. I __________ (couldn't/wouldn't) step out in these heavy rains, if I were you.
2. You __________ (musn't/couldn't) worry about your brother so much. I'm sure he will be all right.
3. You have been unwell for the last two days. You __________ (can/must) go to the doctor.
4. Raj __________ (may/shall) attend the party, but I am not sure.
5. The teacher is never late. She __________ (should/must) have been caught up with something unavoidable.
6. During our childhood, we __________ (must/would) play on the streets all the time.
7. I __________ (can't/mustn't) play the piano. I could never learn it well.

B. Respond to the following situations by using appropriate modals.

1. You have bought a new laptop. Request the cashier for a receipt.

____

____

2. You are caught up with some urgent work. Ask your friend to wait for you.

____

____

3. Ask someone to tell you the time.

4. As a zookeeper, instruct the children not to feed the animals in the cages.

5. Tell your friend that she need not give you a formal invitation for her party.

6. Advise your sister to maintain a regular fitness regime.

7. Request your friend to lend you his pen for writing the exam.

Listening and Speaking

Work in pairs and discuss how some things might make one nervous or scared, but that should not mean they are not fun to try.

You may talk about an incident where you indulged in an adventure sport, like skydiving, or went trekking, with a lot of apprehensions, but later patted your back for being brave.

Pen it Down

Write a diary entry beginning with the given sentence.

It was the middle of a cold December night, and I could no longer ignore the strange sounds coming from the attic, so I...

5
The Road Not Taken

Way with Words

Words with Multiple Meanings

A. Some words have more than one meaning. Frame sentences with two different meanings of the following words. One has been done for you.

1. bolt

   *Jai slid back the **bolt** on the door.*

   *Don't **bolt** your food!*

2. season

   ____

   ____

3. current

   ____

   ____

4. match

   ____

   ____

5. race

   ____

   ____

6. drop

   ____

   ____

7. novel

   ____

   ____

Idioms and Phrases about Choice

B. Match the idioms and phrases about choice with their meanings.

Idioms	Meanings
1. at the crossroads	a. complete something
2. take the first step	b. be in two minds about something
3. come to the end of the road	c. begin a course of action
4. go down that road	d. follow
5. backseat driver	e. be able to adjust to new conditions
6. take the usual path	f. someone who tells others how to do things
7. sea legs	g. initiate a course of action

Grammar in Use

Types of Adverbs

You know that an **adverb** is a word that modifies a verb, an adjective or another adverb.

Read the following sentences to learn about the five types of adverbs.

The little girl danced **gracefully**. (adverb of manner)

Put the box **here**. (adverb of place)

I have a piano lesson **today**. (adverb of time)

I **often** visit my grandparents. (adverb of frequency)

I am **very** grateful to you. (adverb of degree)

Similar to adjectives, adverbs too have three degrees of comparison: positive, comparative and superlative.

The comparative degree of the adverb can be formed by adding **-er** to the base form of the adverb. It can also be formed by adding **more** before the adverb.

Examples: My father walks **fast**, but my brother walks even **faster**.
Heena dances **gracefully**. Maira dances **more gracefully** than Heena.

A. Change the adjectives in the box to their adverb forms. Then, complete the sentences using the comparative form of the adverbs.

regular   old   dark   loud   polite   hard

1. As the storm clouds gathered, it grew ________________ and ________________.

2. If you desire to travel the world, you need to wait till you get ________________

3. They cannot hear you at the back, so you need to speak ____________
4. If you want to succeed, you must work ____________
5. If you wish to earn respect, be ____________ with everyone.
6. If you want to win the game, you need to practise ____________.

Phrases and Clauses

You have learnt that the main difference between a phrase and a clause is that the latter has a verb in it.

Examples: He was **a man of strength**. (Here, 'a man of strength' is a phrase.)
The cat was adopted by a kind gentleman. (This sentence is a clause as it has the verb 'was adopted' in it.)

B. State whether the underlined groups of words are phrases or clauses.

1. If you want to win a medal, you have to practise hard. ____________
2. He worked for me with great dedication. ____________
3. No sooner did I see the time, than I ran for the classroom. ____________
4. The old lady lived in a cottage. ____________
5. She was wearing a dress made of gossamer. ____________
6. San Francisco has a famous bridge. ____________

Listening and Speaking

A. Listen to a poem and answer the questions that follow.

1. How is the world beautifully dressed?

____

____

2. What is the wind occupied with?

____

____

3. Why does the poet refer to the Earth as 'friendly'?

____

____

4. Why is the poet afraid of the Earth sometimes?

____

____

5. Why does the poet think man is God's creation?

____

____

B. Read this poem by W. H. Davies using correct stress and intonation. Then, identify its rhyme scheme.

Sheep

When I was once in Baltimore,
  A man came up to me and cried,
'Come, I have eighteen hundred sheep,
  And we will sail on Tuesday's tide.

'If you will sail with me, young man,
  I'll pay you fifty shillings down;
These eighteen hundred sheep I take
  From Baltimore to Glasgow town.'

He paid me fifty shillings down,
  I sailed with eighteen hundred sheep;
We soon had cleared the harbour's mouth,
  We soon were in the salt sea deep.

The first night we were out at sea
  Those sheep were quiet in their mind;
The second night they cried with fear —
  They smelt no pastures in the wind,

They sniffed, poor things, for their green fields,
  They cried so loud I could not sleep:
For fifty thousand shillings down
  I would not sail again with sheep.

Pen it Down

Write an email to a non-governmental organisation that has done commendable work in rehabilitating the villagers who were displaced due to widespread floods in your state. Besides praising them for their work, volunteer your services for the cause.

____

____

____

____

____

6 A Tale of Two Cities

Comprehension

Read this extract from a story by Subhadra Sengupta carefully and answer the questions that follow.

They had wandered away from the green lawns of the old Residency in Lucknow and now moved deeper into the ruined building. Something dark and fluttering flew past Arjun's face and he ducked nervously, 'What was that? A bat?'

In the fading light, Ira was peering at a small booklet and read out, 'The Siege of the English Residency began after the sepoys of Lucknow revolted on the night of 30 May, 1857. For nearly five months, the sepoys surrounded the Residency and there was fierce fighting. At one time there were nearly 3000 people inside, including officers, soldiers, servants, women and children ...' 'The children began to die first ...' said a quavering voice from somewhere in the gloom behind them, making the three of them jump in fright.

They turned nervously to see a white-haired old man sitting on what looked like a truly antique and very tatty old sofa in the corner. Very, very carefully they went closer to get a better look because the man was quite hard to see in the gloom. Shahid thought that the wavy, grey shadows around him were somehow moving gently and the old man seemed to swim in and out of view.

Ira frowned trying to get a clearer image but the man seemed to be like a reflection in moving water, appearing and disappearing. She couldn't even make out if he was young or old because sometimes the face seemed much younger, at others wrinkled and old. He looked sort of harmless though, leaning on his walking stick and looking up at them with a slight smile.

'Which children?' Arjun asked politely. 'You mean the children in the Residency when the sepoys laid the siege?' 'Correct! The soldiers were dying from bullet wounds and the women and children from cholera, typhoid and small pox.' He gave a shrug. 'Then the food and medicine began to run out. Only a third survived the siege, it was terrible!' Shahid, never too interested in history, decided to change the subject. All the talk of death and dying was getting sort of depressing, 'Well Sir ...' he began, 'Tell me something. After the siege was over, why didn't the people of Lucknow repair this house? Look at the walls and pillars! We need to cement them real fast or they'll collapse any day!'

The old man gave a short laugh, 'The English wouldn't let them. We wanted to keep it exactly the way it was when Sir Colin Campbell arrived with his troops and raised the siege and we could evacuate everyone. We defeated the rebels and this', he waved an arm around him, 'is a monument to our victory. We won!'

They stared at him very puzzled as the image of the man seemed to sharpen a little and Ira looked closely at the ancient face before her. He had a spotty pale skin, a white moustache drooping over narrow lips and a straggly beard. He had a bald head and lines around the eyes; the veined hand was shaking slightly, clasped tightly over the walking stick.

1. Write the meanings of the words as used in the passage.
   a. siege: ______
   b. quavering: ______
   c. evacuate: ______
   d. ancient: ______
   e. clasped: ______
2. Which ancient heritage site had the children been visiting? Where did they wander off?
3. List all the elements that create an eerie atmosphere in that place.
4. Describe the old man in the passage.
5. In not more than 60 words, describe what the old man told the children about the siege and the reason for not repairing the Residency.

Way with Words

Transformation of Parts of Speech

A. Complete the following table.

Noun	Verb	Adjective	Adverb
1. grace			gracefully
2.	energise		
3. beauty			
4.	thank		
5.		cheerful	
6.			briefly

Word Meanings

B. Match the words with their meanings

interpersonal memorise candid competent establish motivation admonish

1. be efficient: ____________________
2. commit to memory: ____________________
3. take to task: ____________________
4. relating to relationships between people: ____________________
5. set up something: ____________________
6. the desire or drive to do something: ____________________
7. be honest and straightforward: ____________________

Grammar in Use

Transformation of Sentences

You know that we can transform sentences in various ways without changing their meanings.

Example: This suitcase is **so** heavy **that** I cannot lift it all by myself.
This suitcase is **too** heavy for me **to** lift it all by myself.

A. Rewrite the following sentences according to the instructions.

1. It is never too late to say sorry. (Use 'so ... that')

2. I was so upset that I could not speak. (Use 'too')

3. You should take an umbrella in case it rains. (Use 'lest')

4. As summer approaches, every student wishes that his or her vacation was longer. (Correct the error in the sentence.)

5. The committee suggested that Justice Kay is chosen as the next Chief Justice. (Correct the error in the sentence.)

6. The bag is not too large to be carried along. (Use 'so ... that')

7. The friends whispered to each other so that they wouldn't be heard. (Use 'lest')

8. She said, 'Leave the hospital immediately!' (Use 'demanded')

9. Anne Frank's family went into hiding so that they were not caught by the Nazis. (Use 'lest')

10. This television is too expensive. We can't afford it. (Use 'too ... to')

11. The minister suggested increasing the tax to meet the growing expenditure of the state. (Use 'so ... that')

12. The box is huge. I can't lift it alone. (Join the sentences using 'so ... that')

13. The principal is very busy. She can't see you now. (Join the sentences using 'too ... to')

14. He is a very proud man. He won't ever ask for help. (Join the sentences using 'so ... that')

ADJECTIVES: CHANGING DEGREES OF COMPARISON

You know that adjectives have three degrees of comparison: positive, comparative and superlative.

Read these sentences.

Arjun had a **clear** look at the man's face. (positive)

Ira frowned trying to get a **clearer** image. (comparative)

Shahid had the **clearest** proof of the matter. (superlative)

Each sentence uses a different degree of comparison for the adjective **clear**.

B. Complete the sentences using the correct form of the adjectives given in brackets.

1. During the race, Usain Bolt was _______________ (fast) than any other athlete.
2. Even the _______________ (mighty) empires cannot escape the ravages of time.
3. The _______________ (powerful) a man is, the _______________ (unhappy) he tends to be.
4. Few other animals are as _______________ (elegant) as the Royal Bengal Tiger.
5. Ram is _______________ (tall) than Laxman but _______________ (short) than Jim, which makes Jim the _______________ (tall) of them all.
6. Being the _______________ (rich) man is _______________ (bad) than being the _______________ (humble) beggar if you are not happy.
7. As the day progressed, the increasingly eccentric behaviour of the Mad Hatter made Alice _______________ (curious).
8. Few other boys are _______________ (hard-working) than Lambert but still he cannot do well in class.
9. This is the _______________ (little) I can do for you.
10. He is the _______________ (good) at what he does but the _______________ (unlucky) when it comes to getting recognition.

Listening and Speaking

Look at the picture and imagine a scene based on it. Describe it in your own words.

You may use the following sentence starters:

- Yesterday, I was standing at...
- There were many...
- However, I didn't see any...
- I was casually roaming when...
- Suddenly, I noticed...

Pen it Down

Which is the most interesting road in your city? Write a descriptive essay on the road. You may include details about its history and significance in the city, and why you like travelling by that road.

7

Ozymandias

Way with Words

Metonymy and Synecdoche

Metonymy is a literary device where an object that is not actually a part of something but is closely associated with it is used for referring to that object.

Example: This **dish** was delicious. (Here, 'dish' refers to the actual food item.)

Synecdoche is a literary device where a part of something is used to represent the whole and vice versa.

Example: India lost by two runs (Here, 'India' is used to represent the Indian cricket team.)

A. Identify the figures of speech used in the following sentences and state whether they are instances of metonymy or synecdoche.

1. Your limbs are alive.

   ____

2. He drank the cup.

   ____

3. You will have the full might of the crown behind you.

   ____

4. The pen is mightier than the sword.

   ____

5. Fill your forms properly if you don't want the suits coming after you.

   ____

6. He earns the bread for the family.

   ____

7. When the convict used his plastic to pay for his ticket, he was caught by the police.

   ____

Words Indicating Size

B. Write the synonyms for 'big' and 'small' in the correct columns. Use a dictionary for the words whose meanings you don't know.

grand minute microscopic vast insignificant expansive paltry stupendous

big	small

Idioms with *Hand* and *Heart*

C. Match these idioms and phrases with hand and heart with their correct meanings.

Idiom/Phrase	Meaning
1. off your hands	a. with a lot of energy and enthusiasm
2. heart and soul	b. do something such as an activity or a sport for the first time
3. out of hand	c. nervous or excited about something
4. try your hand (at something)	d. no longer your responsibility
5. heart in mouth	e. difficult or impossible to control

Grammar in Use

Prepositions

Read the following sentences.

I drew a line **across** the page.

The children were playing **in** the street.

The highlighted words in the above sentences are **prepositions**.

A **preposition** is a word that shows the relation between a noun or a pronoun and other words in a sentence. They can give more information about time, place and movement.

A. Fill in the blanks with suitable prepositions.

1. He dealt ________________ the rogues sternly.
2. That shop deals ________________ wholesale cloth.
3. I wish to dispose ________________ all the old newspapers.
4. Debit cards dispense ________________ the need for cash altogether.
5. I am confident ________________ a resounding victory.
6. I am amazed at his confidence ________________ his team.
7. It is better if you reconcile ________________ your family members.
8. They had no other option but to compromise ________________ their situation.
9. Do you subscribe ________________ the views of this newspaper?
10. Have you paid up your annual subscription ________________ the school magazine?

B. Rewrite the passage after correcting the prepositions that have been used incorrectly.

I am Harsha and I live in Delhi. In monsoon, I like to travel towards Mumbai because from the weather. I just love how it pours at Mumbai. Last summer I flew in Mumbai during June. I went straight of the airport to Marine Drive. Later, we stopped in a coffee shop. We asked our driver to park the car near the shop just in case it pours again. But as luck would have it, the driver parked the car beyond the coffee shop and not close to the front entrance. Finally, we called a local cab and reached the hotel. We were drenched to top from bottom and had our first taste of the rains at Mumbai.

Prepositional Phrases

A **prepositional phrase** is a group of words that functions like a preposition. It consists of two prepositions with a noun in between.

Example: Who is **in charge of** this event?

C. Complete the sentences using the appropriate prepositional phrases given in the box.

at this juncture | in addition to | for want of | in accordance with | in proportion to | on the grounds of

1. He was asked to vacate the premises _______________ inability to pay the rent.
2. The fields dried up _______________ proper irrigation.
3. It is difficult to predict the victory of the team _______________.
4. They were declared husband and wife _______________ the rituals of the community.
5. You must pay a percentage of tax _______________ your income.
6. Do you want me to buy anything else for the party, _____________ what you have written in the list?

Listening and Speaking

The only way to ensure peace is to never hesitate to make war. Do you agree or disagree with this statement? Organise a debate in your class on this topic. Have a show of hands at the end as a quick vote on which side has presented more convincing arguments.

Pen it Down

Imagine that you are an ancient monument. Write an autobiography, mentioning your historical importance and your present condition in not more than 500 words.

Environment

8

The Monk Protectors of Arunachal's Wetlands

Way with Words

Collocations

A **collocation** is a combination of words in a language that occurs quite often and more frequently than would happen by chance.

Examples: I need to **make the bed** every day.
Please **feel free** to take a seat and enjoy the show.

Underline the correct word to complete the collocations in each sentence.

1. How penguins communicate with each other is still a (riddle/mystery/investigation).
2. The terms of the will were (shrouded/covered/hidden) in secrecy.
3. The (location/scene/area) of the crime was cordoned off by the police.
4. The investigations of the (amateur/innocent/unofficial) detective were not given any importance by the police.
5. His new mystery novel met with (wholehearted/pronounced/great) acclaim.
6. In the story, the accused makes some highly (uncanny/damaging/glowing) accusations about the victim.

Grammar in Use

Active and Passive Voice

A sentence in said to be in the **active voice** when the subject is the doer of the action.

Example: My father baked a strawberry cake.

A sentence is said to be in the **passive voice** when the subject of the sentence is the recipient of the action.

Example: A strawberry cake was baked by my father.

When we change a sentence from active to passive, the following changes take place.

1. The subject in the active voice becomes the object in the passive voice. The object in the active voice becomes the subject in the passive voice.
2. The doer of the action may be left out in the passive voice if it is not important. Otherwise, it is preceded by the word *by*.
3. The tense of the verb in the active voice is changed to its appropriate form in the passive.

A. Identify whether the following sentences are in active (A) or passive (P) voice.

1. I was pleased by her progress report. ______
2. Who blew the whistle? ______
3. He was found guilty of theft. ______
4. The house was built by my grandfather. ______
5. They caught the intruder who was hiding in the alley. ______
6. The teacher praised Gautam for his behaviour. ______
7. The manager will give you a free pass for dinner. ______
8. I will do the homework on time. ______

B. Rewrite the following sentences as instructed.

1. The competition was won by the best team. (Change to active voice.)
____
2. The best surgeon in the country performed this surgery. (Change to passive voice.)
____
3. Beethoven composed the Fifth Symphony at the time he was going deaf. (Change to passive voice.)
____
4. Napoleon was defeated by Lord Wellesley in the Battle of Waterloo. (Change to active voice.)
____
5. The dog was given shelter by the kind man on the stormy night. (Change to active voice.)
____
6. J. R. R. Tolkien created a new language while writing *The Lord of the Rings*. (Change to passive voice.)
____
7. *The Dark Knight* trilogy is among the most popular films directed by Christopher Nolan. (Change to active voice.)
____
8. The ancient monument was destroyed by the terrorists. (Change to active voice.)
____

9. The dolphin helped the drowning man reach the shore. (Change to passive voice.)

10. The Persians were routed in the Battle of Plataea by the Greeks. (Change to active voice.)

C. Rewrite the following sentences as instructed.

1. I will pick two hundred pounds of cotton today. (Begin: Two hundred ...)
2. We were invited by the old lady to share some of her food. (Begin: The old ...)
3. Sam promised that he would win the race. (Begin: It was ...)
4. If you disturb the class again, I will write to your parents. (Use 'disturbed'.)
5. The scientist was puzzled by the paranormal activities she witnessed. (Use 'witness'.)
6. People from different countries inhabit India. (Use 'inhabited'.)

Listening and Speaking

Listen to the passage carefully and fill in the blanks.

1. The nuclear arms race began after __________.
2. Environmentalists and peace activists from __________ decided that something more had to be done.
3. These activists believed that __________ was more effective than __________ when it came to confronting difficult issues.
4. The US military were testing __________ on __________ island in Alaska.
5. They chose __________ as the name of their new organisation.

Pen it Down

Read the passage given on page 32 again and write a précis of it. Give it a suitable title.

9 Elder Brother

Way with Words

Synonyms and Antonyms

A. In each set of words, circle the one that is not a synonym of the word in bold.

1. **antique:** traditional, historic, immeasurable
2. **colossal:** gigantic, lavish, mammoth
3. **mocked:** derided, defended, sneered
4. **despair:** anguish, pride, helplessness
5. **command:** order, discipline, neglect

B. Use the antonyms of the following words to complete the sentences.

insensitive	arrived	reject	natural	discontinue	knowledgeable	complicate

1. Mr Smith decided to ____________ the services of his elderly housekeeper as he knew she could not get a job elsewhere.
2. You must ____________ the fact that old age is a difficult time in one's life.
3. Rajesh was ____________ to the needs of his brother.
4. You must ____________ the explanation if you want readers to understand it easily.
5. The plane ____________ as soon as we got off at the airport.
6. I do not like ice creams that have ____________ flavours.
7. Some people prefer to be ____________ of reality rather than face facts.

C. Underline the odd word in each set. Also, say why it is different. One is done for you.

1. vapid, block-head, dense, quirky

   Quirky means eccentric while the others mean unimaginative.

2. caustic, sarcastic, scathing, brash

   ____

3. discourse, admonishment, dressing-down, tirade

____

4. distinguish, determine, cure, detect

____

5. refutation, discredit, invalidate, conflict

____

6. detach, unfasten, disprove, separate

____

7. regard, respect, incompatible, esteem

____

Grammar in Use

Main and Subordinate Clauses

Read this sentence.

Since it was so late, he found it unacceptable to send them all away.

In the above sentence, the group of words in bold forms a **subordinate clause** and the underlined group of words forms the **main clause**.

A **main clause** is a clause that can stand on its own.

A **subordinate clause** is a clause that depends on the main clause to complete its meaning.

A. Underline the subordinate clauses and circle the main clauses in these sentences.

1. The place where we used to go to for holidays is closed now.
2. I don't know who was selected the head prefect.
3. He will only see reason when he speaks to his mother.
4. Although he exercises every day, he has health-related issues.
5. The song which I like has been selected as the theme song of the play.
6. We will go to Jaipur if we get confirmed train tickets.
7. Since Rajiv took my book, I couldn't study for the exam.

B. Add suitable subordinate clauses to complete the sentences.

1. I am sure _______________________________.
2. The house _______________________________ was undergoing repairs.
3. He will participate in the contest _______________________________.
4. _______________________________, he did not perform very well.

5. The mail will arrive ______________________.
6. I like ______________________.
7. This is the place ______________________.

C. Rewrite the following sentences by converting the subordinate clauses to phrases.

1. The boy who is wearing the red t-shirt is my cousin.
____
2. A king who has a kind heart is loved by all.
____
3. He missed the train as he got stuck in the traffic.
____
4. That the Earth is round is a fact accepted by all.
____
5. The criminal lost his head when the famous detective arrived on the scene.
____
6. Only a tiger that has grown old kills humans.
____
7. A diamond that glitters so brightly is sure to attract everyone's attention.
____
8. When we arrived at the hotel, it was already dark.
____

Listening and Speaking

Read the given conversation between two friends.

Friend A: Hello, I heard that your family has moved to a new apartment? Is it comfortable?

Friend B: It is perfect, except that we have a neighbour who is a musician.

Friend A: That's great, right? You love music too. You have something in common to discuss.

Friend B: I don't think so. He bangs on the piano all day making an awful noise. It's worse when his friends come over and they play loud music. There is no peace at home.

Friend A: Well, your parents or you could ask him to use headphones when he practises and request him to soundproof his apartment.

Friend B: But we barely know him and can hardly ask him to stop making a nuisance of himself, can we?

Friend A: Aha! There are other ways …

Continue the conversation in pairs and help Friend B deal with his difficult neighbour.

Pen it Down

Write an argumentative essay on the topic, 'the study of history is necessary in the twenty-first century'. Write your views either for or against the topic, providing suitable examples to support your arguments.

Test Paper

Comprehension

Read this simplified excerpt from *The Diary of Samuel Pepys* about the Great Fire of London that burned down large parts of the city in 1666. Then, answer the questions that follow.

Some of our maids were sitting up late last night to get things ready for our feast the next day. Our maid, Jane, woke us up about three in the morning to tell us of a great fire they saw in the city. So I rose, and went to the window. Being unused to such fires as followed, I thought it far off, and so went to bed again. By and by Jane came and told me that above 300 houses had been burned down by the fire, and that it was then burning down all Fish Street, by London Bridge. So I made myself ready and walked to the Tower; and there got up on one of the high places, and saw that the houses at the end of the bridge were all on fire.

I went down, worried, to the Lieutenant of the Tower, who told me that it began that morning in the King's baker's house in Pudding Lane, and that it had burned St Magnus's Church and most part of Fish Street already. So I rode down to the waterside, and there saw everybody struggling to remove their goods, and flinging them into the river. Poor people stayed in their houses till the fire touched them, and then ran into boats, or clambered from one pair of stairs by the waterside to another. The pigeons too wouldn't leave their houses, but hovered about the windows and balconies, till some of them burned their wings and fell down.

In an hour, I had seen the fire rage every way, and nobody had tried to quench it. I went next to Whitehall (with a gentleman, who wanted to see the fire in my boat). From there, I went up to the King's room in the Chapel, where the people surrounded me. They were very dismayed by my account. I was called to see the King, and told him and the Duke of York that unless His Majesty ordered the houses to be pulled down, nothing could stop the fire. They seemed very worried, and the King commanded me to go to the Lord Mayor, and ask him to spare no houses.

I hurried to St Paul's. Everyone was laden with goods to save and here and there, sick people were being carried away in beds. When I met the Lord Mayor in Cannon Street and gave him the King's message, he cried, 'Lord, what can I do? I am spent. People will not obey me. I have been pulling down houses, but the fire overtakes us faster than we can do it.'

1. Make sentences with the following words, using them differently from the way they have been used in the extract.

   a. fire ____________________

   b. late ____________________

   c. account ____________________

d. spent

e. wings

2. Who informed the narrator about the fire? What information did she provide him later?

3. Where did the narrator head out and whom did he meet? What was he told about the source of the fire and the damage it had done?

4. What did the narrator observe at the waterside?

5. How did the poor people and the pigeons behave during the emergency?

6. Make a list of the words that suggest the panic, fear and efforts of the people to save others and themselves.

Way with Words

A. Choose the correct synonym of the italicised words to complete the sentences.

1. He *clambered* over the slippery rocks as fast as possible. (clawed/swung/jumped)
2. The memory of his past misdeeds *hovered* uneasily in his subconscious as he faced the police officer. (lingered/waited/levitated)
3. Fernando was *dismayed* by the way the boarding school was run by the cruel owner. (perturbed/daunted/awestruck)
4. He *commanded* complete and unquestioning obedience from his band of followers. (instructed/demanded/received)
5. The handloom mills of the village will soon be *overtaken* by the manufacturing factories. (ignored/surpassed/attacked)

6. The proposal presented to the new management committee had no *consequence* (affect/effect/requirement) at all.

B. Create word families for the following words, by writing five words for each.

1. help

   ____

2. write

   ____

3. happy

   ____

4. rain

   ____

5. play

   ____

6. clean

   ____

C. Choose the correct words to complete the idioms in these sentences.

1. All the promises made by the new minister are just ______________ (stars/rockets/pies) in the sky.
2. The amount of money we have collected so far is like a ______________ (fish/drop/turtle) in the ocean compared to the huge amount that we actually need.
3. I had to face the ______________ (pies/stars/music) alone even though everyone was responsible for the broken window.
4. They are not friends anymore. That is why Neelima is giving Paro a cold ______________ (shoulder/handshake/music).
5. His success story is the stuff of fairy tales. You must read about how he went from ______________ (rags/stars/shoulder) to riches.
6. According to Rohan, his entrance exam was a ______________ (pies/piece/slice) of cake.

Grammar in Use

A. Rewrite the following words according to the instructions.

1. Very few subjects are as interesting as English. (Begin: English is ...)

   ____

2. They were being interrogated by the police. (End with 'them')

   ____

3. It is not easy to agree to such a bizarre plan. (Rewrite as a question)

____

4. She has the best headphones I have ever seen. (Rewrite using 'better')

____

5. It is a beautiful outfit. (Rewrite as an exclamatory sentence)

____

6. Lock the gates immediately. (Begin: Let ...)

____

7. Penguins are found only at the South Pole. (Use 'nowhere')

____

8. Not many people agree on the status of Pluto as a dwarf planet. (Use 'few')

____

B. Complete the sentences with suitable prepositions.

1. He has not been getting ____________ well with his new boss.
2. I came ____________ this ancient manuscript by chance.
3. The plane hovered ____________ the mountains before landing.
4. The man sat ____________ the shade of the oak tree.
5. This custom was prevalent ____________ the natives of the region.
6. Gopal is responsible ____________ recruitments in the student cell.
7. The city was ____________ the brink ____________ destruction when the superhero arrived and defeated the villain.
8. After ninety minutes without a goal, the match ran ____________ extra time.

C. Choose the correct options to complete the sentences.

1. The man and his wife ____________ (was/were) given tickets to the concert.
2. You ____________ (would/should) get yourself checked by a doctor.
3. Each boy ____________ (is/are) accountable for his actions.
4. ____________ (Will/May) I have a glass of water?
5. Neither the captain nor the passengers ____________ (was/were) allowed to get off the ship.
6. Each of the passengers ____________ (was/were) given a bottle of water.
7. The teacher, as well as all the children, ____________ (is/are) sitting in the bus right now.
8. Two and two always ____________ (make/makes) four.
9. Every soldier ____________ (is/are) expected to swear allegiance to the country.
10. Bread and butter ____________ (is/are) his staple diet.

11. The students, along with the principal, ____________ (was/were) requested to participate in the contest.

12. The general who commands these soldiers ____________ (is/are) known for his tactical acumen.

D. Identify the words in bold as phrases or clauses.

1. A mountaineer leads a **very interesting** life. ____________
2. The boy **in the blue shirt** is my friend. ____________
3. **If it rains**, we have to go home. ____________
4. The strike carried on **for twenty days**. ____________
5. I first spotted her **when she entered my office**. ____________
6. The boy **who just entered the room** has won a scholarship. ____________
7. The man **who had lost his sight** is being treated by the doctor. ____________
8. The bird **singing outside** my window is a cuckoo. ____________
9. The country **where the city of gold lies** is nothing but a myth. ____________
10. The explorers remained inside their tent with **the wind howling outside**. ____________

Listening and Speaking

A. Imagine that you are a news reporter who witnessed a world record being made at the Tokyo Olympics. Report the action as you saw it unfold before you.

B. Form pairs. Imagine that you are Samuel Pepys and your partner is King Charles II. Inform him about the Great Fire and carry out a conversation on how you plan to prevent the fire from spreading.

You can include the following points in your conversation:

- how much damage has already been done
- the direction in which the fire is spreading
- plans to evacuate the city
- what tools are available to fight the fire

Pen it Down

A. Write an essay discussing some of the ways in which man-made disasters like fire, oil spills, radioactive leakage and contamination can be prevented and dealt with appropriately.

____

____

B. Imagine that you have travelled to the past to meet one of the famous emperors. Whom will you meet? What will you talk about? Write a descriptive essay on the topic.

C. You have read the story, 'The Monkey's Paw'. Write the conversation Mrs and Mr White are likely to have after Mr White used the third and last wish to make their son leave, after the latter had been summoned back to life.

10

The Rime of the Ancient Mariner

Way with Words

Using Give and Take

A. Write sentences using either 'give' or 'take' and a word from those given in the box. One is done for you.

advice	warning	notice	heart	offence	thanks	apart	shape	place	effect

1. *I gave her a warning about her misconduct.*
2. ______________________
3. ______________________
4. ______________________
5. ______________________
6. ______________________
7. ______________________
8. ______________________
9. ______________________
10. ______________________
11. ______________________
12. ______________________
13. ______________________

Archaisms

B. Underline the archaic words used in the following sentences. Write their meanings in the blanks. One has been done for you.

1. Shall I compare *thee* to a summer's day? ___*you*___
2. Give everyman thy ear but few thy voice. __________
3. What good is ye world when ye canst not livest hither. __________

4. Behold her single in the field, / Yon solitary highland lass. __________
5. Whither goest thou, my good man? __________
6. Methinks I shall set up camp here. __________

Grammar in Use

Types of Subordinate Clauses: Adjective, Adverb, and Noun

You know that subordinate clauses are of three kinds:

- A clause that modifies the noun in a sentence is called the **adjective clause**.

  Example: The girl **who is wearing the black dress** is my classmate.

- A clause that modifies the verb, adjective or another adverb in a sentence is called the **adverb clause**.

  Example: I wonder **where they will take us to.**

- A clause that functions as a noun in a sentence is called the **noun clause**.

  Example: Who is going to attend the party is not confirmed yet.

A. Underline the subordinate clause in each sentence and say if it is an adjective clause, a noun clause or an adverb clause.

1. He did what no one could have done. __________
2. Whatever you learn today will help you in the future. __________
3. The book that I want to read will be available in the stores in March. __________
4. Don't go before you meet your friends. __________
5. I will go to the library unless it continues to snow. __________
6. Only the students who have seventy-five per cent attendance will be allowed to take the tests. __________

B. Complete the sentences with the specified clause.

1. ____________________ will win an award. (noun clause)
2. I helped him ____________________ (adverb clause)
3. Do you remember the man ____________________? (adjective clause)
4. Do you know ____________________? (noun clause)
5. My father is the person ____________________ (adjective clause)
6. ____________________, you are safe. (adverb clause)
7. I took a torch with me on my walk, in case ____________________ (adverb clause)

C. Rewrite the following sentences, replacing the underlined phrases with clauses.

1. The woman in the blue suit is the principal of the oldest school in this city.

   ____

2. Neil Armstrong was the first person to step foot on the moon.

   ____

3. Sachin, a humble person, is respected throughout the world as a brilliant batter.

   ____

4. The river flowing through the city is the chief means of transportation for the island dwellers.

   ____

5. *Treasure Island* is a book about an adventurous boy and fearsome pirates travelling together.

   ____

6. All the world is a stage with human beings as the players.

   ____

Complex Sentences

Read the given sentences.

Though she gave no sign, I was sure she had seen me.

Unless I'm mistaken, she was back at work yesterday.

The above sentences are **complex sentences**.

A sentence with one independent or main clause and one or more subordinate clauses is called a **complex sentence**.

D. Join the sentences to make complex sentences. Use the linkers in brackets and make changes as necessary.

1. New Delhi is the capital of India. It is an ancient city as well. (which)

   ____

2. Many multinational companies have their headquarters in New Delhi. There are still a large number of underdeveloped areas. (although)

   ____

3. You are late for school. Can you give me a valid reason? (why)

   ____

4. The boy hid the jewel. No one would find it. (where)

   ____

5. Jake was late for school. He had missed the bus. (because)

   ____

6. You study for the exam. You will fail. (unless)

____

7. The person helped the accident victims. He is my classmate. (who)

____

Listening and Speaking

We scan a poem by dividing it into 'feet', pointing out different accented and unaccented syllables. We then identify its metre. The most famous example of poetic metre is iambic pentameter, which is an unstressed syllable followed by a stressed syllable.

A. Read these three stanzas from the poem 'Stopping by Woods on a Snowy Evening' by Robert Frost. Look at the first stanza, which has been scanned. The stressed syllables are marked with an apostrophe. Each foot is separated by a stroke (/) and the syllables are separated using a hyphen. Now scan the remaining two stanzas.

Whose woods'/ these are'/ I think'/ I know'/
His house'/ is in'/ the vil'/-lage though;'/
He will'/ not see'/ me stop'/-ping here'/
To watch'/ his woods'/ fill up'/ with snow.'

My little horse must think it queer
To stop without a farmhouse near
Between the woods and frozen lake
The darkest evening of the year.

He gives his harness bells a shake
To ask if there is some mistake.
The only other sound's the sweep
Of easy wind and downy flake.

B. Divide the class into groups of equal number and play the game of Spin-a-Yarn. Start with the prompt 'The clock had just struck twelve when ...'

You can use the following points in your story:

- It was a cold dark night ...
- The moon had just come out ...
- The last thing she saw was ...

Pen it Down

Ending a story can be more difficult than beginning it. Keep in mind the following ideas while deciding a perfect ending for the story you are writing:

- Make it sensible, not predictable.
- Allow room for the reader's interpretation.
- Remember the theme of your story.
- You may include a surprise or a plot twist.

Read the given sentences. Write an account of what you think happened next. Give a suitable title to your story.

Ricky wants to be a dancer. Although his mother is supportive of his choice, she asks him to focus on his studies. Ricky decides to follow his passion while also obeying his mother ...

11 The Six Napoleons

Comprehension

Read this extract from the story *The Secret Garden* and answer the questions that follow.

Aristide Valentin, Chief of the Paris Police, was late for his dinner, and some of his guests began to arrive before him. Valentin's house was an old house, with high walls and there was no exit at all except through this front door, which was always guarded.

When Valentin arrived, he saw his principal guest was not there. He saw all the other invited guests. He also saw a tall man in uniform, Commandant O'Brien, of the French Foreign Legion. When he bowed to the Ambassador's family, Lord and Lady Galloway, bent stiffly, and Lady Margaret looked away.

Valentin was expecting a man of world-wide fame, Julius K. Brayne, the multi-millionaire. The solid appearance of Brayne in the room was as decisive as a dinner bell. He had this great quality, that his presence was as big as his absence. He was a tall fellow, clad in complete evening black.

Except on one point, the Galloways were casual enough. So long as Lady Margaret did not take the arm of O'Brien, her father was quite satisfied; and she had not done so. She had gone in for dinner with Dr Simon. Nevertheless, old Lord Galloway was restless and almost rude. When after dinner he saw that Commandant O'Brien was absent, and that Lady Margaret was absent too, he stamped along the passage. As he went towards the back of the house, where Valentin's study was, he was surprised to meet his daughter, who swept past with a white, scornful face, which was puzzling. If she had been with O'Brien, where was O'Brien! If she had not been with O'Brien, where had she been?

Lord Galloway made his way to the dark back parts of the mansion, and eventually found a servants' entrance that opened on to the garden. The silver light lit up all four corners of the garden. A tall figure in blue was striding across the lawn towards the study door; a glint of moonlit silver on his face picked him out as Commandant O'Brien.

He vanished through the French windows into the house, leaving Lord Galloway in an indescribable temper.

The length and grace of the Irishman's stride enraged him. He stepped briskly after his enemy. As he did so he tripped over some tree or stone in the grass; looked down at it first with irritation and then a second time with curiosity. The next instant the moon and the tall poplar trees looked at an unusual sight – an elderly English diplomat running hard and crying or bellowing as he ran.

His hoarse shouts brought a pale face to the study door, the beaming glasses and worried brow of Dr Simon, who heard the nobleman's first clear words. Lord Galloway was crying: 'A corpse in the grass – a blood-stained corpse.'

'We must tell Valentin at once,' said the doctor, 'It is fortunate that he is here,' and even as he spoke the great detective entered the study, attracted by the cry. It was almost amusing to note his typical transformation; he had come with the common concern of a host and a gentleman, fearing that some guest or servant was ill. When he was told the gory fact, he turned with all his gravity instantly bright and business like; for this, however abrupt and awful, was his business.

'Strange, gentlemen,' he said as they hurried out into the garden, 'that I should have hunted mysteries all over the earth, and now one comes and settles in my own backyard. But where is the place?' They crossed the lawn less easily, and found the body sunken in deep grass – the body of a very tall and broad-shouldered man.

'At least,' said Simon, with a deep and singular intonation, 'he is none of our party.' 'Examine him, doctor,' cried Valentin rather sharply. 'He may not be dead.' The doctor bent down. 'He is not quite cold, but I am afraid he is dead enough,' he answered.

– G. K. Chesterton

A. Answer these questions in brief.

1. Who was the principal guest of Aristide Valentin? Describe him.

___

2. Who was Lady Margaret? Who was her dinner companion?

___

3. Why did Lord Galloway stamp along the passage?

___

4. What was the second mystery for Lord Galloway?

___

5. What happened in the garden after O'Brien left it?

___

6. How did Valentin's manner change when he saw the corpse?

___

B. Match the words in column A with their antonyms in column B.

A	B
1. guarded	a. flexibly
2. stiffly	b. calm
3. solid	c. unreliable
4. decisive	d. clear
5. restless	e. unprotected

C. Answer these questions with reference to context.

1. *Valentin's house was an old house...*
   a. Who is Valentin?
   b. What do we learn about his old house?
   c. What was taking place in this old house?

2. *Except on one point, the Galloways were casual enough.*
   a. Who were the Galloways?
   b. What was the one point on which they were not casual enough?
   c. What is the meaning of 'casual' in the context of the above sentence?

3. *'We must tell Valentin at once,' said the doctor, 'It is fortunate that he is here;'*
   a. Why was the doctor relieved at Valentin's presence?

b. What did Valentin see in his own backyard?

____

____

c. Why did Valentin ask the doctor to examine the body again?

____

____

Way with Words

Words from Detective Fiction

A. Complete the paragraph using the words in the box.

genres	investigator	thrilling	deduction	clues	intellectual
crime	motives	mystery	suspense	suspects	

Detective fiction has remained as one of the most popular ____________ of writing. In a detective story, the reader is challenged to solve the ____________ by following the ____________ provided by the writer. The reader follows the adventures of the ____________ whose great powers of observation and ____________ make him superior to the criminal who has executed a seemingly perfect ____________. A challenging detective story has a variety of ____________ with different ____________. These stories are full of ____________ and often end in a ____________ manner. It has been rightly said, 'The detective story is a kind of ____________ game.'

Types of Books

B. Read the clues and fill in the blanks using the words in the box.

folktale	historical fiction	fantasy	dystopian fiction	thriller

1. the setting of this type of book is a society which is worse than the one you live in ____________
2. the plot of this type of book is inspired by legends and folklore ____________
3. this type of book or story uses clues and red herrings, and may end in a cliff-hanger ____________
4. the characters in this type of book are partly real and can also be found in history books ____________
5. this type of book or story is usually set on another planet ____________

Grammar in Use

Direct and Indirect Speech

When we refer to the exact words of the speaker in a sentence, it is said to be in **direct speech**.

Example: Mohit said to Rishi, 'What are you doing tomorrow?'

When we report what somebody said or thought in our own words, we use **indirect speech**.

Example: Mohit asked Rishi what he was doing the next day.

When a sentence is written in indirect speech, the tense, pronouns, modals, reporting verbs and indicators of time and place change.

Convert the sentences from direct speech to indirect speech and vice versa.

1. 'Why are you wasting your time with this video game?' my mother asked me.
2. I was advised two weeks bed rest by the doctor.
3. 'Hurrah! We have won the tournament,' shouted the team members of the women's hockey team.
4. Huma mentioned that she had to return the library book that week.
5. 'I had enough of this drama today and I am going to get myself a cup of coffee,' announced Paro.
6. Ram informed his mother that he would reach home late that night.
7. They remarked, 'Your group has put up an extraordinary performance.'
8. He said, 'I have done remarkably well in these semester exams, Mother.'
9. Veena told us that she was extremely glad to be with us last evening.
10. Grandmother told us to sit quietly and observe the customers.

Listening and Speaking

Listen to an extract from Arthur Conan Doyle's *The Hound of the Baskervilles* carefully. Then choose the correct answers.

1. Sherlock Holmes' visitor had left behind ____________________.
   a. a letter
   b. a walking stick
   c. an identification document
   d. a doctor's prescription
2. Holmes wanted Watson to examine the walking stick and deduce ____________________.
   a. the visitor's name
   b. the visitor's occupation
   c. the visitor's home address
   d. the reason for the visit
3. Watson's first observation was that the visitor was ____________________.
   a. a country medical practitioner
   b. a town doctor
   c. a detective
   d. an athlete
4. Watson concluded that the owner of the stick was ____________________.
   a. successful, elderly and well-esteemed
   b. tired and hungry after a long journey
   c. a man of many talents and abilities
   d. a friend of Holmes
5. Holmes appreciated Watson for ____________________.
   a. being modest about his own abilities
   b. having great intellect
   c. lending him money when he was in debt
   d. being an energetic walker

Pen it Down

Imagine you are walking down the corridor of a museum when suddenly one of the exhibits starts moving. Write a short story on what happens next. Give the story a suitable title.

Sport

12

The Commentator

Way with Words

Idioms with *Talk*

A. Here are some idiomatic expressions with the word talk. Match the expressions in column A with their meanings in column B.

A	B
1. money talks	a. have knowledge about something from your own experience
2. now you're talking	b. used to tell somebody that they should not criticise others for something that they also do
3. know what you're talking about	c. people who have a lot of wealth have more power and influence than others
4. look who's talking	d. say something that you should not because it is the wrong situation or it offends somebody
5. talk out of turn	e. used when you like what somebody has suggested very much

Words Related to Football

Read these words related to football and their meanings.
linesmen: assistant referees who stand beside the line of the field or pitch and keep an eye on the players from that view
midfielders: players positioned between the defenders and forwards on a field
These terms refer to specific roles or positions in a game of football. Several such terms are used in football.

B. Complete the passage with football terms from the box.

linesmen	midfielders	extra time	free kick	penalty shoot-out

The goalkeeper was tense as the referee had awarded a ________________ to the opponents. Messi took his position while the ________________ also kept an eye on the game from the side-lines. So far the match had been a well fought one and the ________________ did a good job on the pitch. There was a chance that the match would go into the ________________ if Messi did not score. Even after that, there was a chance of a ________________ to decide the draw.

Grammar in Use

Tenses

You know that tenses refer to present, past and future time. They take four forms: the simple, the continuous, the perfect and the perfect continuous.
Study the given table to learn about the different tenses.

simple present tense	The monkey **eats** a banana.
simple past tense	The monkey **ate** a banana.
simple future tense	The monkey **will eat** a banana.
present continuous tense	The monkey **is eating** a banana.
past continuous tense	The monkey **was eating** a banana.
future continuous tense	The monkey **will be eating** a banana.
present perfect tense	The monkey **has eaten** a banana.
past perfect tense	The monkey **had eaten** a banana.
future perfect tense	The monkey **will have eaten** a banana.
present perfect continuous tense	The monkey **has been eating** a banana.
past perfect continuous tense	The monkey **had been eating** a banana.
future perfect continuous tense	The monkey **will have been eating** a banana.

Rewrite the sentences using the correct tense of the underlined verbs.

1. Tory is <u>studied</u> for the exam as we speak.

____

2. She was never late for classes. I wonder what is kept her now.

3. I was slept all day yesterday.

4. Sara lost her temper at little things. She trying to restrain herself.

5. The store opened at 10 a.m. and closed at 9 p.m. every day.

6. Listen! Someone was playing the flute so beautifully.

7. While we enjoyed ourselves in the open, it started pouring.

Listening and Speaking

Work in pairs. Enact a conversation in which one of you apologises to the other for not being able to help with the classwork owing to lack of time.

You may use the following points in your conversation:

- the pressure of completing assignments on time
- no time after school because of football practice
- any other way one could help the partner

Pen it Down

A. Imagine that you participated in an inter-school basketball tournament and played an important role in helping your team win the trophy. Write a paragraph, including details about the different teams, your contribution to the tournament and how your actions helped your school win the coveted trophy.

B. Your school is organising the annual sports day. Make a poster inviting the students. Mention the date, time, and venue, and give it a suitable heading. Also mention that Olympic gold medallist Neeraj Chopra is going to grace the event with his presence as the Chief Guest.

13 The Gift of the Magi

Comprehension

Read the story and answer the questions that follow.

At Denver there was an influx of passengers into the coaches on the eastbound B. & M. Express. In one coach there sat a very pretty young woman dressed in elegant taste. Among the newcomers were two young men, one of handsome presence with a bold, frank countenance and manner; the other a ruffled, glum-faced person, heavily built and roughly dressed. The two were handcuffed together.

As they passed down the aisle of the coach, the only vacant seat offered was a reversed one facing the attractive young woman. Here the linked couple seated themselves. The young woman's glance fell upon them with a distant, swift disinterest; then with a lovely smile she held out a little grey-gloved hand. When she spoke her voice, full, sweet, and deliberate, proclaimed that its owner was accustomed to speak and be heard.

'Well, Mr Easton, if you will make me speak first, I suppose I must. Don't you ever recognize old friends when you meet them in the West?'

The younger man roused himself sharply at the sound of her voice, seemed to struggle with a slight embarrassment which he threw off instantly, and then clasped her fingers with his left hand.

'It's Miss Fairchild,' he said, with a smile. 'I'll ask you to excuse the other hand; it's otherwise engaged just at present.'

He slightly raised his right hand, bound at the wrist by the shining 'bracelet' to the left one of his companion. The glad look in the girl's eyes slowly changed to a bewildered horror. The glow faded from her cheeks. Her lips parted in distress. Easton, with a little laugh, as if amused, was about to speak again when the other forestalled him. The glum-faced man had been watching the girl's countenance with veiled glances from his keen, shrewd eyes.

'You'll excuse me for speaking, miss, but, I see you're acquainted with the marshal here. If you'll ask him to speak a word for me when we get to the pen, he'll do it, and it'll make things easier for me there. He's taking me to Leavenworth prison. It's seven years for counterfeiting.'

'Oh!' said the girl, with a deep breath and returning colour. 'So that is what you are doing out here? A marshal!'

'My dear Miss Fairchild,' said Easton, calmly, 'I had to do something. Money has a way of taking wings unto itself, and you know it takes money to keep step with our crowd in Washington. I saw this opening in the West, and took it.'

'That's wonderful! And so now you are one of these dashing Western heroes, and you ride and shoot and go into all kinds of dangers. That's different from the Washington life. You have been missed from the old crowd.'

The girl's eyes, fascinated, went back, widening a little, to rest upon the glittering handcuffs.

'Don't you worry about them, miss,' said the other man. 'All marshals handcuff themselves to their prisoners to keep them from getting away. Mr Easton knows his business.'

'Will we see you again soon in Washington?' asked the girl.

'Not soon, I think,' said Easton.

'I love the West,' said the girl irrelevantly. Her eyes were shining softly. She looked away out the car window. She began to speak truly and simply without the gloss of style and manner: 'Mamma and I spent the summer in Denver. She went home a week ago because father was slightly ill. I could live and be happy in the West. I think the air here agrees with me. Money isn't everything. But people always misunderstand things and remain stupid –'

'Say, Mr Marshal,' growled the glum-faced man. 'This isn't quite fair. I'm needing a drink, and haven't had a smoke all day. Haven't you talked long enough? Take me in the smoker now, won't you? I'm half dead for a pipe.'

The bound travellers rose to their feet, Easton with the same slow smile on his face.

'I can't deny a petition for tobacco,' he said, lightly. 'It's the one friend of the unfortunate. Good-bye, Miss Fairchild. Duty calls, you know.' He held out his hand for a farewell.

'It's too bad you are not going East,' she said, 'But you must go on to Leavenworth, I suppose?'

'Yes,' said Easton, 'I must go on to Leavenworth.'

The two men sidled down the aisle into the smoker.

The two passengers in a seat nearby had heard most of the conversation. Said one of them: 'That marshal's a good sort of chap. Some of these Western fellows are all right.'

'Pretty young to hold an office like that, isn't he?' asked the other.

'Young!' exclaimed the first speaker, 'Why – Oh! Didn't you catch on? Say – did you ever know an officer to handcuff a prisoner to his right hand?'

A. Answer these questions.

1. On which coach were the passengers travelling?

____

2. Where had Miss Fairchild first met Mr Easton?

____

3. What crime did the glum-faced man say he had committed?

____

4. Where did Miss Fairchild say she wanted to live?

____

5. Where was Mr Easton going?

____

B. Answer these questions with reference to context.

1. *'It's Miss Fairchild,' he said, with a smile. 'I'll ask you to excuse the other hand; it's otherwise engaged just at present.'*

   a. Who is Miss Fairchild talking to?

   ____

   b. Describe the initial reaction of Miss Fairchild on seeing the two men.

   ____

   ____

   c. Which hand did the speaker offer Miss Fairchild? What excuse did he give for being unable to use his 'other hand'?

   ____

   ____

   d. What did the glum-faced man say about the marshal?

   ____

   ____

2. *Said one of them: 'That marshal's a good sort of chap. Some of these Western fellows are all right.'*

   a. Who is the speaker and his companion?

   ____

   b. Who is the marshal in the story? What is the convict being punished for?

   ____

   ____

   c. What important information does the speaker give on the handcuffs attached to Mr Easton and his companion?

   ____

   d. What role do the speaker and his companion play in this story?

   ____

C. Choose the correct words to complete the idioms.

1. He could not find it in his __________ (heart/hand) to refuse the children a trip to the park that afternoon.
2. I like to keep my dictionary at __________ (heart/hand) when I write an essay.
3. He knew the area like the back of his __________ (heart/hand) and could give perfect directions when asked.
4. The minister was determined to get to the __________ (heart/hand) of the matter before the meeting ended.
5. The defending champion set her __________ (heart/hand) on emerging victorious despite her injury.

6. After the match, it was discovered that the player was ________ (hand/heart) in glove with the referee.

Way with Words

Idioms Related to Money

A. Match these idioms associated with money with their meanings.

Idiom	Meaning
1. bring home the bacon	a. pay excessively for something
2. cash in one's chips	b. pay for something
3. pay a king's ransom	c. sell something to fund something else
4. live from hand to mouth	d. earning a salary
5. foot the bill	e. to be challenged by someone
6. get a run for their money	f. make do with the bare minimum

B. Use the idioms from exercise A to complete the following sentences. You may have to make necessary changes.

1. I work hard throughout the week to ________________.
2. She ________________ and funded the education of the children of the refugee camp.
3. Who will ________________ for these lavish parties?
4. The singers ________________ when the wild card entrant impressed all the judges.
5. I ________________ to go on a world tour this year.
6. Due to the coronavirus pandemic and loss of jobs, many are ________________.

Suffixes

C. Add suitable suffixes to the words in brackets and complete the sentences.

1. The leaves of certain trees are ________________ (poison) for cattle.
2. We were somewhat amazed to enter a ________________ (spot) and clean courtyard.
3. There was an explosion of ________________ (scholar) interest in her poetry.
4. The weather is very ________________ (change) at this time of year.
5. Gurjit wants to be a famous ________________ (mathematics) when he grows up.
6. The roads outside our colony were so narrow that the municipal corporation had to ________________ (wide) them.
7. Stop this ________________ (silly) and get back to work!

Grammar in Use

USING *FOR*, *DURING* AND *WHILE*

Read the following sentences. Note the use of **for, while** and **during** to denote time.
I'm going away **for** a few days.
You can go swimming **while** I'm having lunch.
There are extra flights to Finland **during** winter.

A. Rewrite the following sentences after correcting the incorrect use of for, while and during.

1. The match has been going on during one hour and still nobody seems to have the upper hand.
2. During you were playing football, we finished our homework.
3. The streets were waterlogged as it had rained heavily for the night.
4. It will take us four hours while completing this task and then we will be free.
5. Some people spend their life dreaming during others try to realise their dreams.
6. No one is allowed to go out while the screening of the film.
7. For my brother is enjoying his holiday, I have been working on this project while the last three months.
8. You should start preparing for the exam during there is still time.

QUESTION TAGS

Read the following sentences. Notice that a positive statement is followed by a negative question tag, while a negative statement is followed by a positive one.
He is coming to the party, **aren't he?**
You did not tell me the recipe, **did you?**

B. Complete the sentences with suitable question tags.

1. We are all working on the project together, _______________?
2. It will be very difficult to convince her, _______________?
3. We finished our work on time, _______________?
4. She doesn't want to go out to the park in this rain, _______________?
5. The construction workers usually finish the drilling at 5 p.m., _______________?
6. You must apologise for your conduct, _______________?
7. We can't leave the baby alone, _______________?
8. Your cousin isn't married, _______________?
9. We will see you tomorrow, _______________?
10. They shouldn't stand too close to the water's edge, _______________?
11. Let's try to call her again, _______________?
12. They really maintain their garden well, _______________?
13. She's the best singer in our class, _______________?

Subordinating Conjunctions

Read the following sentence.
The man was fined **because** he violated the traffic rules.
Here, the highlighted word is a **subordinating conjunction**. It defines the cause-and-effect relationship between the main clause (*the man was fined*) and the dependent clause (*he violated the traffic rules*).

A **subordinating conjunction** is a word or phrase that connects a dependent clause to the main or independent clause. It also adds information to the sentence, indicating the relationship between the two clauses.

After, although, as, as if, as long, because, before, by the time, if, in order that, in case, lest, only if, provided that, though, unless, until and **when** are examples of subordinating conjunctions.

C. Join the following pairs of sentences using suitable subordinating conjunctions.

1. It was raining. We did not go out to play.

   ____

2. The sun set. The cattle returned home.

   ____

3. He is shy. He is a talented singer.

   ____

4. We were reminded that it was Martyrs' Day. They did not want us to forget.

   ____

5. You can read. You have time till the library closes at 8 p.m.

   ____

6. Batman drove his bat mobile. It took him quickly to the scene of crime.

Listening and Speaking

Listen to a passage on the Statue of Liberty and answer the following questions.

1. Which two countries shared a strong bond of friendship?

2. Who was the chief architect of the Statue of Liberty?

3. Why were various fundraising options considered?

4. What made Pulitzer's ploy a success?

5. Why couldn't Bartholdi execute his incredible idea ?

Pen it Down

A. Write a review of the book *Born Free* by Joy Adamson.

Remember to include the following points in your review:

- name of the author
- date of publication
- gist of the novel
- theme and plot
- setting
- characters
- interesting highlights
- style
- what you liked about the novel
- something that can be improved in the novel

B. **Write an alternate ending for one of your favourite fairy tales.**
You could change the climax and the actions of the different characters that contribute to the climax. You may also add a few characters to enable the change that you wish to bring about.

Man and Nature

14 The Last Wolf

Way with Words

Contextual Usage

A. Fill in the blanks using the words in the box.

muzzle	whining	warrens	rubble	highrises	baying

1. The corrupt lawyer seems to be ____________ for the blood of the poor and innocent defendant.
2. The ____________ of the gun was still smoking hot when it was located at the scene of the crime.
3. There is no use ____________ and complaining about the poor quality of food at roadside eateries.
4. After the enemy jets bombed the city, the entire landscape was just a sad pile of ____________.
5. Spiderman can easily find his way through the ____________ of the New York cityscape.
6. There is no need to build more ____________ in a city so prone to earthquakes.

Idioms Related to Animals

B. Match the idioms related to animals with their meanings.

Idiom	Meaning
1. cried wolf	a. very hot days
2. cat nap	b. gave a false alarm
3. to chicken out	c. tackle a situation
4. dog days	d. opt out due to fear
5. made a beeline for	e. short sleep
6. to take the bull by its horns	f. headed straight for

C. Fill in the blanks using the idioms you just learnt.

1. It was shocking to see the volunteers ______________ at the last minute from the project.
2. Please let me take a quick ______________ as I am exhausted after last night.
3. These ______________ in summer seem to last forever.
4. The children ______________ for the front row seats at the magic show.
5. It is time ______________ and tackle the pandemic on a war footing.
6. The woman ______________ so often that when she really needed help, the security company took their time to come to her aid.

Grammar in Use

JOINING SENTENCES: PARTICIPLES

Read the following sentences.

He trotted across the floor.

He laid his long grey muzzle on the spare white spread.

The above sentences can be joined and rewritten as:

Trotting across the floor, he laid his long grey muzzle on the white spread.

The word **trotting** is a **present participle**. It can be used to join two simple sentences whose subject is the same and in which the actions (**trotted** and **laid**) are happening at the same time.

A. Join the given pairs of sentences as instructed.

1. The king was warned of the imminent revolt. He escaped the city. (begin with 'Being …')

   ____

2. The thirsty crow saw the pot of water. It began to throw pebbles in it. (begin with 'Seeing …')

   ____

3. He gave up investing in quick money-making schemes. He had lost a lot of money. (begin with 'Having …')

   ____

4. They were harassed by some goons. They complained to the police. (begin with 'Being …')

   ____

5. The passenger alighted from the plane. He tripped on his bag. (begin with 'Alighting …')

   ____

6. The magician took pity on the dove. She set it free. (begin with 'Taking …')

   ____

B. Join these sentences using present participles and rewrite them.

1. They are vegans. They don't eat meat, dairy and other animal products. (begin: Being ...)
2. We met a girl. She was carrying a bouquet of flowers. (use 'carrying')
3. He loudly knocked at the gate. He demanded admission. (use present participle of 'knocked')
4. The man sat in the library. He was reading a book. (use 'sitting')
5. Riya walked home. She met an old friend. (Use present participle of 'walked')
6. Mr Sinha was occupied with work. He had no time for the meeting. (Begin: Being...)
7. I saw the sun rise. I opened the window. (Being: Seeking ...)
8. He seized the keys. He rushed to the door. (Begin: Seizing ...)

Listening and Speaking

Divide the class into two groups and have a discussion on the topic 'Conservation is survival'. Bring forth interesting viewpoints connected to this topic. Try to be objective and focus on making an impact and offering actionable points.

Pen it Down

Write a newspaper report on an amazing scientific invention that has taken the world by storm. Remember the more fantastical the invention you describe, the more fun it will be. Give a suitable and catchy headline to your report.

15 A Short Walk in the Hindu Kush

Comprehension

Read the extract from *The Adventures of Huckleberry Finn* and answer the questions that follow.

I had decided to go the circus. I made sure nobody saw me when I sneaked into the circus and loafed around the back side till the watchman went by, and then dived in under the tent. I had my twenty-dollar gold piece and some other money, but I reckoned I better save it, because there is no telling how soon you are going to need it, away from home and amongst strangers that way. You can't be too careful. I am not opposed to spending money on circuses when there is no other way, but there is no use in wasting it on them.

It was the splendidest sight that ever was when they all come riding in, two and two, a gentleman and lady, side by side, and dressed in clothes that cost millions of dollars, and just littered with diamonds. It was a powerful fine sight; I never seen anything so lovely. And then one by one they got up and stood, and went a-weaving around the ring so gentle and wavy and graceful, the men looking ever so tall and airy and straight, and the women looking lovely.

And then faster and faster they went, all of them dancing, first one foot out in the air and then the other, and the clown cracking jokes; and by and by all hands dropped the reins, and every lady put her knuckles on her hips and every gentleman folded his arms, and then how the horses did lean over! And so one after the other they all skipped off into the ring, and made the sweetest bow I ever see, and then scampered out, and everybody clapped their hands wildly.

Well, all through the circus they did the most astonishing things; and all the time the clown carried on with his entertaining jokes. As soon as the ringmaster said a word to him, he was back at him quick as a wink with the funniest things anybody could ever say; and how he ever could think of so many of them, was what I couldn't understand.

And by and by a man tried to get into the ring – said he wanted to ride; said he could ride as well as anybody that ever was. They argued and tried to keep him out, but he wouldn't listen, and the whole show come to a standstill. Then the people began to holler at him and make fun of him, and that made him mad. So, then, the ringmaster he made a little speech, and said he hoped there wouldn't be no disturbance, and if the man would promise he wouldn't make no more trouble, he would let him ride if he thought he could stay on the horse. So everybody laughed and said all right, and the man got on. The minute he was on, the horse begun to jump and run around, with two circus men hanging on to his bridle trying to hold him, and the man hanging on to his neck, and his heels flying in the air every jump, and the whole crowd of people standing up, shouting and laughing till tears rolled down. It wasn't funny to me, though; I was fearing for the man's safety. But pretty soon he grabbed the bridle, and the next minute he sprung up on the horse and dropped the bridle and stood! Finally the man made his bow and danced off to the dressing-room, and everybody laughed with pleasure.

The ringmaster had got up that joke all out of his own head, and never let on to anybody. I felt sheepish to have been fooled, but I wouldn't have been in that ringmaster's place, not for a thousand dollars. I don't know; there may be bigger circuses than this one, but I had never seen a better one. I decided then I would never miss an opportunity to spend my money on such a show again.

A. Answer these questions with reference to context.

1. *I sneaked into the circus and loafed around the back side till the watchman went by.*
   a. Who is the speaker?
   ____
   b. Why did he loaf around the back?
   ____
   ____
   c. What did he do after the watchman went by?
   ____
   ____
2. *... and how he ever could think of so many of them, was what I couldn't understand.*
   a. Who is the *he* in these lines?
   ____
   b. What is being referred to as *so many of them*?
   ____
   ____
   c. What could the speaker not understand?
   ____
   ____

B. Answer these questions.

1. Describe the sight of the men and women on horses.
   ____
   ____
2. What does the narrator feel about the clown? Write in three sentences.
   ____
   ____

3. Does the narrator like the ringmaster? Support your answer with sentences from the passage.

____

____

4. How did the man fool the narrator?

____

____

5. Explain the line: *'I felt sheepish to have been fooled.'*

____

____

6. Why does the narrator finally decide that it is worth spending money on a circus?

____

____

C. Read the given meanings. Write the words associated with them in the blanks.

sneaked	weaving	skipped off	standstill	bridle	reckoned

1. guessed ____________
2. the headgear used to control a horse ____________
3. the action of forming a pattern by interlacing something ____________
4. a complete stop ____________
5. moved in a stealthy way ____________
6. left a place quickly or in a secret way ____________

Way with Words

CONTEXTUAL USAGE

A. Fill in the blanks using suitable words from the box.

recital	diplomat	haze	inquisitive	suffocation	distinguished

1. The prolonged bush fires created a ____________ of clouds around the city for some days.
2. The Chief Guest had a rather ____________ appearance and spoke eloquently.
3. The ____________ was recalled to his country after allegations of spying were made against him.
4. The President gave a ________ at the beginning of the programme.
5. The feeling of ____________ increased as smoke filled the room.
6. Children are ____________ by nature and like asking questions.

Compound Adjectives

Read the following sentences.

He is a **well-known** actor.

My grandfather went for a **much-delayed** medical check-up.

The highlighted words in these sentences are **compound adjectives**.

A **compound adjective** is an adjective that is made up of two or more words.

B. Complete the sentences with appropriate compound adjectives.

long-standing	last minute	second-class
record-breaking	duty-free	world-famous

1. Several discounts are available if you make ________________ reservations with the airline.
2. There was a ________________ agreement between Sarah and her mother that after she finished college they would go on a world tour.
3. The wrestler had many ________________ achievements in his long career.
4. Adil bought an expensive bottle of perfume for his mother from a ________________ shop at the Delhi Airport.

5. They planned a day trip to the ________________ horticultural gardens on the last day of their holiday.
6. We decided to forego our trip to Pondicherry because only ________________ train tickets were available.

Grammar in Use

Infinitives and Gerunds

You know that we can join sentences using infinitives and gerunds.

Examples:

1. I am going to Mohini's house. I will study there.
   I am going to Mohini's house **to study**. (infinitive)
2. I meditate every day. It keeps me calm.
   Meditating every day keeps me calm. (gerund)

A. Join the following sentences using infinitives where necessary.

1. He was sensible. He made all the arrangements.

2. I would rather starve. I would not eat such oily food.

3. The burglar took out the dagger. He wanted to frighten us.

4. She did nothing else. She only cried.

5. The syllabus is too lengthy. It cannot be covered in a week.

6. I am happy. You have invited me to the inaugural ceremony.

7. He is too lazy. He will not be able to finish the work on time.

8. Our opponents are too strong. We will not be able to play an attacking game.

B. Replace the infinitives in the following sentences with gerunds.

1. To persevere is better than to laze around.

2. To write is not a difficult pursuit.

3. She loved to paint and to dance.

4. Try to jog half an hour every day if you want to stay fit.

5. The only way out of the mess is to apologise.

6. To brush twice a day is important for dental hygiene.

7. To cook was the first household skill that Ravish learned.

8. To forgive is a divine act.

Listening and Speaking

What would a conversation between two people from absolutely different cultures be like? Form pairs and carry out such a conversation.

You may use the following points:

- the similarities in the cultures
- the things that set them apart
- what is unique about each culture
- appreciation for a different culture

Pen it Down

A. Look at the following images. Now, write a story that links all the four images.

1. 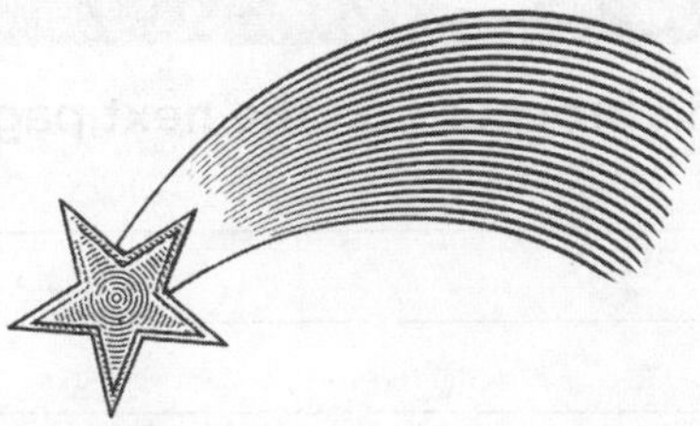	3. 
2. 	4. 

B. Prepare a travel brochure for an exotic destination. Your travel brochure must contain the following information.

- location of the destination
- means of transport to get there
- best time to visit the place
- attractions
- accommodation
- food
- contact details
- relevant pictures

Make short notes in the space given below and design the brochure on the next page.

16

Refugee Blues

Way with Words

Using Suffixes to Form Nationalities

You have learnt that suffixes are used to form names of different nationalities.

Examples:

-ian: Indian, Canadian

-ean: Korean, Chilean

-an: Jamaican, Cuban

-ese: Balinese, Chinese

-ic: Icelandic, Arabic

-ish: English, Finnish

-i: Iraqi, Afghani

A. Add the correct suffixes to the names of the countries to form nationalities.

Country	Nationality
1. Guatemala	
2. Indonesia	
3. Bangladesh	
4. Japan	
5. Malta	
6. Estonia	
7. Egypt	
8. Ireland	
9. Nepal	
10. Poland	

Words of Foreign Origin

B. Match the words of foreign origin in column A with their meanings in column B.

A	B
1. annum (Latin)	a. summary
2. ennui (French)	b. year
3. résumé (French)	c. unplanned
4. ad hoc (Latin)	d. genuine
5. bona fide (Latin)	e. boredom
6. modus operandi (Latin)	f. goodbye
7. ensemble (French)	g. method
8. adieu (French)	h. group

Grammar in Use

Determiners: Quantifiers and Distributives

Quantifiers refer to numbers or quantity. They can be used with both countable and uncountable nouns.

Examples: We don't have very **many** copies left.
There was so **much** traffic that we were an hour late.

Distributives are used to refer to a group of people or things, or to individual members of the group.

Examples: She knows **every** student in the school.
Neither answer is correct.

A. Complete the sentences using the words given in the box.

least	less	later	much	more	many	every	either	neither

1. Winning the tournament should be the ____________ of your worries.
2. ____________ child was given a book of wizarding rules.
3. We have ____________ volunteers but not ____________ enthusiasm.
4. ____________ actor can fit the part well.
5. I'm disappointed because ____________ of the two dresses matches what I had in mind.
6. The former suggestions of the board had been rejected unlike the ____________ ones.
7. The ____________ we have, the ____________ content we are.

PUNCTUATION

B. Rewrite the sentences using proper punctuation.

1. an ex student of this institution went on to become the twenty third president of the country
2. when he left his job it was twelve years ago he was just a trainee
3. i am not really sure what is to be done he stammered
4. how the mighty have fallen
5. isnt it her mother who won the booker prize last year
6. marks a historian he lives in an eighteenth century house

7. all species of tigers especially those from south china are endangered
8. rahul likes I wonder why all dishes consisting of bitter gourd
9. aditya an enthusiastic mountaineer is planning to go to the himalayas next year

Listening and Speaking

Listen to the passage carefully. State whether the given sentences are true (T) or false (F).

1. Samuel's family was lost in the flood. ☐
2. World leaders have been able to control the number of displaced people living in their countries. ☐
3. Catastrophic weather disasters create climate refugees. ☐
4. Climate change is a localised phenomenon. ☐
5. Most climate refugees cannot return home when conditions change. ☐

Pen it Down

A. Write a newspaper report on the dangers refugees face while attempting to flee a land of conflict. Use information available in the print or digital newspaper that you read every day to write the report.

Your report should contain the following details:

- the countries of origin and the countries to which the refugees have migrated
- the cause of the strife
- the condition of the refugees
- some refugee profiles
- efforts to solve their problems

B. **Write a poem on the theme of displacement. Use a refrain to express your feelings on this topic. You may also work in a group. You can use a refrain either in the form of a line or a stanza that emphasises the theme of the poem.**

Humour

17

My Financial Career

Comprehension

Read this extract from *Don Quixote* and answer the questions that follow.

At this point they came in sight of thirty or forty windmills that there were on that plain, and as soon as Don Quixote saw them he said to his squire, 'Fortune is arranging matters for us better than we could have ourselves, for look there, friend Sancho Panza, where thirty or more monstrous giants present themselves, all of whom I mean to engage in battle and slay, and with whose spoils we shall begin to make our fortunes; for this is righteous warfare, and it is God's good service to sweep so evil a breed from off the face of the earth.'

'What giants?' said Sancho Panza.

'Those thou seest there,' answered his master, 'with the long arms, and some have them nearly two leagues long.'

'Look, your worship,' said Sancho; 'what we see there are not giants but windmills, and what seem to be their arms are the sails that when turned by the wind make the millstone go.'

'It is easy to see,' replied Don Quixote, 'that thou art not used to this business of adventures; those are giants; and if thou art afraid, away with thee out of this and go pray while I engage them in fierce and unequal combat.'

So saying, he, kicked his horse Rocinante on the side and started, heedless of the cries his squire Sancho sent after him, warning him that most certainly they were windmills and not giants he was going to attack. He, however, was so positive they were giants that he neither heard the cries of Sancho, nor saw, near as he was, what they were, but rushed at them shouting, 'Fly not, cowards and vile beings, for a single knight attacks you.'

A slight breeze at this moment sprang up, and the great sails began to move, seeing which Don Quixote exclaimed, 'Though ye have more arms than the giant Briareus, ye have to reckon with me.'

So saying, and swearing his love for his lady Dulcinea, imploring her to support him in such a peril, with lance in rest and covered by his buckler, he charged at Rocinante's fullest gallop and fell upon the first mill that stood in front of him; but as he drove his lance-point into the sail the wind whirled it round with such force that it shattered the lance to pieces, sweeping with it horse and rider, who went rolling over on the plain, in a sorry condition. Sancho rushed to his assistance as fast as his ass could go, and when he came up, found him unable to move, with such a shock had Rocinante fallen with him.

'God bless me!' said Sancho, 'did I not tell your worship to mind what you were about, for they were only windmills? and no one could have made any mistake about it but one who had something of the same kind in his head.'

'Hush, friend Sancho,' replied Don Quixote, 'the fortunes of war more than any other are liable to change often; and moreover I think, and it is the truth, that that same sage Friston who carried off my study and books, has turned these giants into mills in order to rob me of the glory of defeating them, such is the enmity he bears me; but in the end his wicked arts will do but little against my good sword.'

'God order it as he may,' said Sancho Panza, and helping him to rise got him up again on Rocinante, whose shoulder was half out; and then, discussing the late adventure, they followed the road to Puerto Lapice.

'I believe it all as your worship says it; but straighten yourself a little, for you seem all on one side, may be from the shaking of the fall.'

'That is the truth,' said Don Quixote, 'and if I make no complaint of the pain it is because knights-errant are not permitted to complain of any wound, even though their insides are coming out through it.'

'If so,' said Sancho, 'I have nothing to say; but God knows I would rather your worship complained when anything ailed you. For my part, I confess I must complain however small the ache may be; unless this rule about not complaining extends to the squires of knights-errant also.'

Don Quixote could not help laughing at his squire's simplicity, and he assured him he might complain whenever and however he chose, just as he liked, for, so far, he had never read of anything to the contrary in the order of knighthood.

– *Miguel de Cervantes*

1. **Read these sentences and state whether they are true (T) or false (F).**
   a. Don Quixote believed that giants were an evil breed. ☐
   b. Don quixote asked Sancho Panza to pray for him as he fought the giants. ☐
   c. Don Quixote's horse refused to charge the windmills. ☐
   d. Don Quixote's lance was shattered to bits by the moving arms of the windmills. ☐
   e. Sancho Panza could not see the giants as they were hidden behind the windmills. ☐
   f. Don Quixote said that the sage had changed the windmills into giants to trick him. ☐
   g. Don Quixote warned Sancho Panza not to complain about his own injuries as it was against the code of knighthood. ☐

2. *'Hush, friend Sancho,' replied Don Quixote, 'the fortunes of war more than any other are liable to change often.'*
   a. Who was Sancho Panza? Where were they going?

   ____

   ____

b. What war had Don Quixote just fought? What was the outcome of this war?

c. Who did Don Quixote blame for the outcome of the war? Why?

d. What help did Sancho Panza offer him?

e. Why, according to Don Quixote, couldn't Sancho Panza see the windmills? What kind of relationship did he share with his master?

3. Use these words from the passage to make sentences in which they have a meaning different from that in the passage.

a. long:

b. shivered:

c. order:

d. sweeping:

e. rule:

Way with Words

IDIOMS RELATED TO ANXIETY

A. Read the following idioms related to anxiety, along with their meanings.

Idiom	Meaning
1. be on the edge of one's seat	be tense about something
2. have butterflies in the stomach	be nervous
3. blood run cold	be very frightened
4. with bated breath	almost holding one's breath in anticipation
5. be a bundle of nerves	be very nervous and worried
6. shaking like a leaf	trembling in fear

Now fill in the blanks using the idioms you have just learnt. You may have to make some necessary changes.

1. The thought of meeting the world champion made Aamir a ________________, so that he couldn't even tie his shoelaces properly.
2. We waited for the announcement of the results ________________.
3. We got ________________ the moment we heard that there would be a surprise math test today.
4. Everyone in the audience was ________________ while watching the risky performance of the trapeze artists.
5. The shriek of the banshee made our ________________ and a chill ran down our spine.
6. The poor student was ________________ while he was appearing for his practical examination.

SIMILAR SOUNDING WORDS

Words which sound similar but are different in spelling and meaning, are called **homophones**.

Example: altar (meaning 'shrine') and **alter** (meaning 'to change')

B. Fill in the blanks with the correct word pairs.

cheque – check	compliment – complement	carat – carrot	led – lead

1. a. The diamond was priced highly for its ___________ value.
   b. The rabbit munched on its ___________ inside the cage.
2. a. The ___________ for illegal substances at airports was made more thorough.
   b. Have you cashed the ___________ at the bank?

3. a. One must __________ others for their achievements.
   b. The team needs players who __________ each other.
4. a. She __________ the team from the front throughout the match.
   b. A harmful percentage of __________ was found in the drinking water of the village well.

Grammar in Use

TRANSFORMATION OF SENTENCES

Rewrite the following sentences according to the instructions.

1. As soon as the rain began, the peacocks started dancing. (Begin: No sooner ...)

   ____

2. Despite the warnings, the people continued to litter the roads. (Begin: Although ....)

   ____

3. If you leave immediately, you will be able to catch the 3 o'clock train to Lucknow. (Use 'unless')

   ____

4. She is too young to be part of the team. (Remove 'too')

   ____

5. India is the largest democracy in the world. (Begin: No other ...)

   ____

6. She did not forget to take her medicines. (Use 'remember')

   ____

7. Despite the rough weather, they set sail. (Begin: In spite of ...)

   ____

8. Even though the accommodation was terrible, we enjoyed the wedding. (Use 'although')

   ____

9. The car is economical. It's great to drive. (Use 'not only ... but also ...')

   ____

10. I will call you the minute I wake up. (Begin: As soon as ...)

    ____

11. I am too tired to go for a jog. It is raining too. (Use 'besides')

    ____

12. She has three dogs. She has two cats too. (Use 'besides')

    ____

Listening and Speaking

Listen to the passage carefully and choose the correct options.

1. How long had Jimmy Valentine been in prison?
   a. ten months b. four years
   c. a year d. a day
2. Why was Jimmy in prison?
   a. for making bad shoes b. for cracking safes
   c. for having a good heart d. for being unemployed
3. What advice did the warden give Jimmy?
   a. to brush up on his skills b. to lead an honest life
   c. to leave the prison the next morning d. to wear new clothes
4. What provisions did the state not give Jimmy when he left the prison?
   a. a railway ticket b. a snack
   c. an ill-fitting suit d. a pardon
5. What character trait does Jimmy Valentine not show in this extract?
   a. a friendly and carefree nature b. a criminal mentality
   c. being a hardworking person d. a confident and breezy manner

Pen it Down

Write down the process of getting vaccinated in the backdrop of the COVID-19 pandemic. Remember to list the stages clearly and in the correct order. Also mention any complications that might arise. Make sure you use transition words to link the different steps of the process.

18 The Tragedy of Julius Caesar

Way with Words

Irony

Irony is a figure of speech in which the real meaning of the words is the opposite of what is said.

Example: 'But Brutus says he was ambitious;
And Brutus is an honourable man.'
The use of 'honourable man' is ironical as Antony is trying to prove that Brutus is not being honourable or truthful.

A. Explain the irony in the following situations.

1. When the exiled minister returned to his country, his first words were, 'It is great to be back.' Then, he was arrested.

 ____

2. He looked through the window where it was pouring outside and said, 'Now that's a great day!'.

 ____

3. The police station was robbed at night.

 ____

4. No sooner did the car leave the car wash than it began to rain heavily.

 ____

5. *The Titanic*, which sank on its first voyage, was thought to be an 'unsinkable' ship.

 ____

Archaic Sentences

B. Rewrite the following lines in contemporary English.

1. When that the poor have cried, Caesar hath wept:

 ____

2. O masters, if I were disposed to stir/Your hearts and minds to mutiny and rage

____

3. Let but the commons hear this testament—

____

4. It will inflame you, it will make you mad:

____

5. I have o'ershot myself to tell you of it:

____

Understatement

An understatement is a figure of speech used by writers or speakers to intentionally make a situation seem less important than it really is.

C. Match the expressions below with their meanings.

Understatement	Implied meaning
1. I am afraid you have made quite a mess of things.	a. It was a total disaster, we deserved to lose!
2. Well, he is not really one of my favourite people.	b. Oh! You have totally ruined everything!
3. The team did not perform as expected today, and the better team won.	c. Pay up!
4. I would appreciate it if you could return my money as soon as it suits you.	d. Srinivasa Ramanujan was a mathematical genius.
5. Srinivasa Ramanujan had a good head for numbers.	e. It rained heavily. The roads are flooded.
6. It looks like it rained a bit last night. The cars are under water.	f. I can't stand him!

Grammar in Use

Simple, Compound and Complex Sentences

Sentences are of three types, based on structure. They are simple, compound and complex sentences.

A **simple sentence** has a subject and a finite verb. It makes complete sense on its own.

Example: Read the will.

A **compound sentence** has two or more independent clauses. They are joined by a coordinating conjunction.

Example: Then follow me, **and** give me audience.

A **complex sentence** contains a main clause and at least one subordinate clause. The subordinate clause depends on the main clause for meaning and cannot stand on its own.

Example: **If** thou consider rightly of the matter, Caesar/has had great wrong.

Here, the underlined words form the subordinate clause, while the remaining words form the main clause.

A. Rewrite the following sentences according to the instructions.

1. The building was damaged in the earthquake. The family was saved. (Join without using 'and', 'but' or 'so').

2. He looked behind. He saw the policemen following him. (Begin: Looking ...).

3. He was hardworking. He was enthusiastic. (Use 'Not only ... but also ...').

4. The people with the most power are the ones with the most drive. (Use 'who').

5. He escapes. He dies in prison. (Use 'either').

6. Brian spoke. He seemed to be a born orator. (Use 'when').

7. Search his pocket. I am sure you will find the ring. (Use 'if').

8. He worked very hard. He won against all odds. (Use 'so that').

9. The baby was rocked by her mother. She continued to cry. (Use 'although').

10. Listen carefully and I will tell you a secret. (Use 'if').

____

11. I am glad that he has shown good progress. (Use 'and').

____

12. He studied in a Bengali-medium school and he learned to speak Bengali there. (Use 'where').

____

Joining Sentences with Correlative Conjunctions

Correlative Conjunctions are sets of conjunctions which are used together for joining words, phrases or two sets of independent clauses.

Example: She is intelligent. She is compassionate.
She is **both** intelligent **and** compassionate.
Some other correlative conjunctions are **neither...nor, either ...or, hardly had... when, no sooner...than, whether...or.**

B. Join the following pairs of sentences using correlative conjunctions.

1. Caesar was ambitious. Caesar was generous.

____

2. I did not attend class today. My best friend did not attend class today.

____

3. You can go out to play. You can complete your homework.

____

4. The little girl saw her mother. She started smiling.

____

5. The captain got a bout of food poisoning. The goalkeeper also got a bout of food poisoning.

____

6. The insect sat on the leaf of the Venus flytrap. The leaf closed.

____

7. He is a poet. He is a playwright.

____

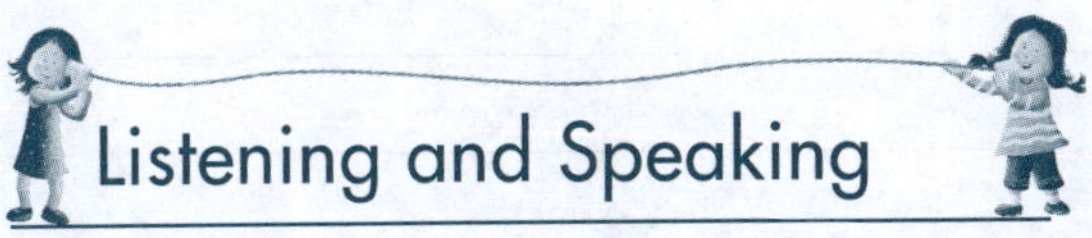

Listening and Speaking

Recite the speech made in the play, *The Tragedy of Julius Caesar* by Marc Antony, 'Friends, Romans, countrymen, lend me your ears'. Then, explain its meaning in your own words.

Pen it Down

A. As the Head Boy/Head Girl of your school, write a speech you have been asked to make on the rising incidents of bullying on campus.

You can include the following points in your speech:

- examples of bullying you have witnessed
- your sympathy and solidarity with the bullied
- what solutions you have to offer

B. Imagine that your school is organising week-long art classes by a famous painter. Write a notice asking the students to take part in the classes, mentioning the location, date and time.

You can include the following points in the notice to draw the students' attention:

- the name of the painter
- the different painting techniques he/she would teach

Assessment

Comprehension

Text A. Read the passage and answer the questions that follow.
We are all aware of the need to shift to a greener economy that is low in carbon emissions. This passage discusses the toll on the environment caused by internet usage and how we can do something about it.

Our society has become digital to a point where, without a smartphone or a computer, our capacity to do anything is severely restricted. It is estimated that the internet represents more than 1% of the world's energy consumption, an amount greater than the total consumption of several nations combined.

The amount of water required to produce appropriate hydroelectric power equals the amount of water it would take to fill one million Olympic-sized swimming pools per year. The space needed to house the hard-drive equipment in the 'data centres', with all our e-mails, photos, videos, files and documents, adds up to an area that equals the size of New York City, Rio de Janeiro and Mexico City combined.

The number of daily internet users around the world is about 900,000. All that usage has to be powered somehow, and in a world where more than 84% of its energy is sourced from fossil, it is not a small thing.

Big companies like Microsoft, Google, Facebook, and Apple have committed to using 100% renewable sources of energy and lowering their emissions by the end of the decade. But even renewables like the energy produced at hydroelectric plants has a big carbon footprint.

With a few changes in our individual use of the internet, we can lower our impact in a significant way. For example, decreasing the resolution from HD to standard while streaming videos, would reduce these emissions significantly. In the same way as we are rejecting single-use plastics, doing more recycling and composting, or using electric vehicles, these simple digital habits will save our environment.

Questions

1. Choose the most appropriate meaning of the word 'restricted' as used in the passage. (1 mark)

   a. limited b. restrained

2. Choose the most appropriate meaning of the word 'consumption' as used in the passage. (1 mark)

   a. eating habits b. utilisation

3. Explain the meaning of the following sentences:

   a. *Big companies like Microsoft, Google, Facebook, and Apple have committed to using 100% renewable sources of energy.* (2 marks)

   b. *All that usage has to be powered somehow, and in a world where more than 84% of its energy is sourced from fossil, it is not a small thing.* (2 marks)

4. What is meant by the phrase 'rejecting single-use plastics'? (2 marks)

5. Is this extract written in formal or informal language? Give two instances to support your response. (2 marks)

6. What role does the mentioning of statistics play in the extract? (2 marks)

7. Do you think it will be possible to reduce carbon emissions by following digital protocols? (3 marks)

Text B. Read this extract from *The Ransom of Red Chief* by O. Henry and answer the questions that follow. The story follows two kidnappers who steal Johnny, the son of a rich man. The son, called Red Chief by the kidnappers, is a redheaded, devilish brat. He makes life miserable for the two criminals. This extract talks about the ransom demand sent to Red Chief's father and the father's reply.

Ebenezer Dorset, Esq.: We have your boy concealed in a place far from Summit. It is useless for you to get the most skilful detectives to attempt to find him. This is your only way to get him back. We demand fifteen hundred dollars for his return; the money to be left at midnight tonight at the same spot and in the same box as your reply. If you agree to these terms, send your answer by messenger tonight at half-past eight o'clock. After crossing Owl Creek, on the road to Poplar Cove, there are three trees, close to the fence of the wheat field. At the bottom of the fencepost, opposite the third tree, will be found a small pasteboard box. The messenger will place the answer in this box and return immediately to Summit. If you pay the money as demanded, he will be returned to you safe and well within three hours, otherwise you will never see him again. This is our final communication.

TWO DESPERATE MEN.

Two Desperate Men

Gentlemen: I received your letter, in regard to the ransom you ask for the return of my son. I think you are a little high in your demands, and I hereby make you a counter-proposition, which I think you will accept. You bring Johnny home and pay me two hundred and fifty dollars in cash, and I agree to take him off your hands. You had better come at night, for the neighbours believe he is lost, and I couldn't be responsible for what they would do to anybody they saw bringing him back.

Very respectfully,

EBENEZER DORSET.

Questions

1. Locate the correct answers in the passage. (4 marks)

   a. What was Johnny's current location?

   b. By what time did the messenger have to leave his message?

   c. Where would the small pasteboard box be found?

   d. How much money did Ebenezer demand of the kidnappers?

2. Choose the correct answers. (3 marks)

a. Ebenezer would see his boy again if he ________________.

i. spoke to his neighbours

ii. paid the ransom on time

iii. asked the detectives to look for him

iv. made a counter-proposition

b. Ebenezer did not agree to the kidnappers' demands because ____________.

i. the neighbours would be angry with him

ii. they refused to pay him two hundred and fifty dollars in cash

iii. they agreed to come at night

iv. their demands were too high for him

c. Ebenezer wanted Johnny to be returned at night because ________________.

i. he was concerned about Johnny's safety

ii. the kidnappers were far away from Summit

iii. the neighbours would punish the kidnappers for returning Johnny

iv. he felt responsible for his son's disappearance

3. Explain the irony behind the father asking for money from the kidnappers for his son's return. (2 marks)

____

____

____

____

4. The word 'desperate' can refer to a feeling of hopelessness or a deep desire for something. Which meaning is more suited to describe these two men? Give two reasons for your answer. (2 marks)

____

____

____

____

5. Why do you think Ebenezer is convinced that his counter-proposition will work? (2 marks)

____

____

____

____

6. How do you think the kidnappers will respond to this letter? (2 marks)

____

____

____

NOTES